WHAT TO DO
WHEN YOU CAN'T
DECIDE

MEG LUNDSTROM

WHAT TO DO
WHEN YOU CAN'T
DECIDE

USEFUL TOOLS FOR FINDING
THE ANSWERS WITHIN

SOUNDS TRUE

BOULDER, COLORADO

Sounds True, Inc.
Boulder CO 80306

Book design by Lisa Kerans
Interior photos by Michael Meyers
Cover illustration based on an image by Merkushev Vasiliy/
Shutterstock

Printed in Canada

Library of Congress Cataloging-in-Publication Data
Lundstrom, Meg.
  What to do when you can't decide : useful tools for finding the
answers within / Meg Lundstrom.
      p. cm.
  Includes bibliographical references (p. 297) and index.
  ISBN 978-1-59179-816-3 (pbk.)
  1. Divination.   I. Title.
  BF1751.L86 2010
  133.3--dc22
                                    2010001649

10 9 8 7 6 5 4 3 2 1

I dedicate this book to you, the reader.
May it bring you what you need at this moment
in the dynamic dance of the One.

To Sandra, even The
Voice of sage counsel
and compassion!
Much love to you,
with hopes of seeing
you soon,

Meg

CONTENTS

LIST OF ILLUSTRATIONS

INTRODUCTION

What should I do?
Is this good for me or not?
Which one do you recommend?
How do I get out of this fix?
Should I keep going in this direction?
Is there a better way for me to do this?

When we have pressing questions and don't know which way to turn, we naturally ask them of someone in the know—our parents, our friends and teachers, or experts such as doctors, lawyers, and financial advisors. Depending on their expertise and insight, the outcome might work out—or not.

But in just this way, we can tap a deeper, wiser source. We can ask simple, direct questions of that underlying essence of life, love, and wisdom that is called by many names: God, our higher self, higher consciousness, Pervasive Unity, Presence, the superconscious, the Universe. By using a simple, convenient physical object—such as our fingers, a pendulum, or folded pieces of paper—we can get a clear-cut Yes/No answer. Astonishingly, the response turns out to be just what we need. It weighs factors we have no conscious knowledge of, bypasses unanticipated obstacles, and fast-forwards us on the path to greater clarity and love.

Historically, this process is known as divination. The word comes from the Latin *divinus,* meaning belonging to or relating to a deity—and when divining is done with care and reverence, it leads us ever more deeply into our innate divinity. (In this book, the word "divining" is used. "Divination" implies a system, whereas "divining" speaks to the dynamic, unfolding, in-the-moment, collaborative nature of asking for and receiving guidance.)

Divining can be used in matters large and small—choosing a dentist or a destination, selling a house or an idea, devising a job shift or a shopping list, diving into our limiting beliefs or a new relationship.

As practical as divining is for even mundane decisions, at its heart it is a spiritual process—spiritual as opposed to material, in the sense that something is happening that can't be explained by your five senses. How is it that when you ask the question, the right answer comes? Where does the answer come from? There are many explanations, all of them a matter of belief. What is wonderful, however, is that divining requires no particular belief for it to work, just the ability to take a deep breath and jump in. The results will be in the immediate feedback you get—the appointments that fall flawlessly into place, the turn in the road that saves you from a traffic jam, the job or house that turns out to be exactly what you need.

It is also spiritual in the way that it leads you directly into your own profound depths. Divining helps you open up to the latent wisdom within yourself. It is through your own firing neurons, through your own muscular system, through the immense panorama of your own unconscious, that the answers arrive. Although there are some useful guidelines, the process is customized by you, and through it you will find yourself experiencing not only the vast potential of life, but the responsiveness of the Universe. The Divine—however you conceive of it—is waiting to give you what you need, and these tools are simple means to figure out what that is.

WHAT YOU'LL FIND HERE

This book differs from other books on divining because it focuses on three simple, direct tools for making a decision: muscle-testing, or kinesiology, which uses muscle strength in your fingers as a marker; pendling, or asking questions using a pendulum; and the chits, a randomized casting of lots that uses folded pieces of paper. These are systems of inner guidance that give you Yes/No answers without much "story" or interpretation; in fact, you'll have a hard time *not* understanding the answer. These methods differ from the *I Ching* and Tarot, for example, which are symbolic systems based on metaphor and open to wide interpretation.

Also, the three tools in this book lend themselves to use on mundane as well as weighty questions. They are portable. They are so direct that the biggest challenge may well be not how to use them, but how not to overuse them.

If you've never divined before, this book lays out the landscape so you can choose what works for you and attain precise, useful results in a short time. If you've dipped into divining now and then—maybe you have a pendulum sitting in a drawer somewhere—you'll learn systematically how to improve your results so that you move fully and exuberantly through the world, even when the going gets tough. And if you're already accomplished at divining, the creativity of divining experts interviewed for this book may inspire you to try new approaches and lines of questioning.

The emphasis in this book is on decision-making in the moment. It is not on fortune-telling. Here is the difference: I might ask what is the best day to take a trip to Chicago or what flight is the best one to take there; however, I won't ask if I'll meet a business opportunity on that flight. Making decisions opens doors; fortune-telling subtly closes them. More often than not, attempting to peer into the future produces wrong or erratic results—because it is often not in our best and highest interest to know what is coming around the bend, as much as the managing mind may want advance notice.

This book is about decision-making for you alone, not for others. You'll learn as you work with these tools about your own blocks and hidden assumptions, and gentle guidance will come your way over time to move past them. But performing muscle-testing, pendulum-dowsing, or chit-tossing for others entails major karmic responsibility and should not be undertaken until you, first of all, have your own practice well in hand, and second, get further training from experts who will help you identify any blockages. You'll find suggestions in this book on how to get that additional training.

In part 1, you'll learn about the benefits, history, and science of the divining tools taught in this book. You'll see how divining is a play of consciousness that you can shape to fit your own needs.

In part 2, you'll first find step-by-step instructions for muscle-testing and pendling, tools that share many features in their application and lend themselves to on-the-spot responses. You'll learn not just the mechanics, but the all-important procedures for entering a receptive inner state, getting yourself out of the way, asking the question clearly, and assessing the result. You'll see how you can hone in on information and, in the advanced chapters, you'll learn how to expand the range and depth of the simple Yes/No response through creative lines of questioning and dialoguing. In chapter 10 you will read about the chits, which require little skill-building and are useful for weightier, emotion-prone questions. A walk-through of some supplementary approaches is also included should you want to delve deeper into the underlying dynamics, the whys and wherefores, of a situation.

The epilogue ponders larger questions about the divining process: Can we go beyond choice? Who, actually, is framing the question and doing the choosing? And what comes first, the question or the answer?

In the appendixes, you'll find a Divining Checklist, which is a troubleshooting guide to help you identify and move through any difficulties you might experience with a tool. There is also an annotated bibliography for further exploration.

WHY I WROTE THIS BOOK

I'm not an impersonal observer of these tools: I've used them for two decades, and they have shaped my life by giving me direction and courage. I find that divining stirs something deep within me—gratitude, connectedness, unity, as if all walls are down between me and the forces that move the Universe. The answers feel right, uncanny in a way if I stand back and look at them, but correct and even inevitable, like the next step in a dance I'm remembering how to do. It's out of gratitude for the discovery and delight that have resulted from my divining that I wrote this book.

To better understand how divining works, I searched out and interviewed thirty-six experts and practitioners. Some were teachers from the American Society of Dowsers (ASD), who use hand tools to expertly find hidden things ranging from underground water veins to lost cats. Some were skillful instructors of muscle-testing, others health practitioners who use it with patients. Several are friends in the Catskills who started using muscle-testing years ago; with each of them it has evolved differently, so you'll see just how individualized the process can be. Some are serious meditators at ashrams in India who divine to keep their mind free of clutter, and some are ordinary, everyday people who divine to make their lives focused and efficient. (If interviewees gave permission for their names to be used, their full names are included. If they chose to be anonymous, only a first name is used, which is a pseudonym.)

I've also examined the literature to come up with the basics for beginning a divining practice, yet many of the most practical suggestions have come from the hands-on experiences of the interviewees.

My divining has often directed me to India for spiritual teachings, a path foretold by my favorite library book as a ten-year-old, accounts of the lives of Hindu, Buddhist, Muslim, and Taoist children. I wrote much of this book on a long sojourn in India and Nepal; many of my personal examples come from that time. Your path most likely is different, and the divining process is custom-tailored to meet each person's unique needs.

One important point: this book is a work in progress, not a gospel. It is only the best understanding I have acquired to date from my experiences and the wisdom of the people I've interviewed, and much remains to be learned. As you put your own fingerprints on your divining process, you can help stretch the boundaries. By being both creative and rigorous, you can add to the collective wisdom on the subject.

May this book be helpful to you in moving in harmony with the deepest currents in yourself and the Universe, which are one and the same.

PART ONE

WHAT DIVINING IS

CHAPTER 1

DIVINING

HOW IT WORKS AND WHAT IT CAN DO FOR YOU

Do you find yourself constantly puzzling, even agonizing, over the choices you have to make on a daily basis? Does the "tyranny of small decisions," as economists term it, leave you stymied when you face a shelf of similar sunscreen products, a complex chart of cell-phone plan options, or a long list of health-care providers? Does the terror of large decisions—what to do for a living, whom to live with, where to live, how to respond to changing circumstances—leave you confused and paralyzed?

Or maybe you're making decisions easily enough, but you're often unhappy with the outcome. After spending time and energy carefully thinking something through, you belatedly learn that you did not adequately research and weigh all the options. Or perhaps the outcome was affected by factors that hadn't even occurred to you at the time. Perhaps you bumped up against the limitations of your mind, conditioned by your upbringing and experiences to ignore some input and magnify others. Maybe you're seeing that you make the same poor choices over and over. Maybe fear of the future limits your view of what is possible, so you mistakenly rule out good options.

And perhaps you regret the roads and risks not taken for reasons that now seem beside the point.

From work to romance to finances, there has never been a more complex society for the average person to negotiate. And although it would seem that more choices mean more freedom, the sheer number of alternatives in itself is stressful, say psychologists. Studies show that feeling inner pressure to make the best possible decision leads to anxiety, regret, confusion, and lower self-esteem.[1] In fact, too many choices mean that "choice no longer liberates, but debilitates. It might even be said to tyrannize," writes psychologist Barry Schwartz in *The Paradox of Choice: Why More Is Less.* And if the opposite happens—your choices seem to shrink due to factors outside your control—frustration and fear can overpower your rational mind and block your intuition, short-circuiting your ability to find good solutions.

Don't despair. Divining is another way to make decisions—and it allows you to bypass the ruts of your mind and the dictates of your emotions in order to come up with creative choices that work out astonishingly, unexpectedly well. It allows you to tap into the part of yourself that is wiser, calmer, and all-knowing.

It is a guidance system that is easy, immediate, and accessible. All it requires is for you to take a leap of faith—small or large, depending on your beliefs—and try it out. You simply ask a question, use one of the tools in this book, and await the answer. It comes instantly, just like that.

You can use divining for everything from scheduling appointments to choosing a job or house—and beyond, into deep inner processes. These tools will take you however far you are willing to go. Divining for the highest good—the prerequisite—may well increase your happiness, prosperity, and comfort. But ultimately, it opens you up to letting go of your preconceived needs, and that, in turn, creates a space for the Divine to step in and give you gifts beyond description.

Like life itself, divining is not static or fixed or set in concrete; rather, it's a dynamic, deeply personal process that ebbs, flows, and changes over time. Learning to move with it becomes a graceful dance with the Universe. Just as when you learn the tango or the trombone, the more you practice with divining tools, the better you'll get and the more your ease and confidence will grow. You'll find the rhythm that suits you: using it daily or rarely, as a solo strategy or in concert with research, intuition, and advice seeking.

If at times the divining guidance feels a little scary, that is good. It means you are moving beyond your narrow self-conceptions and the mental wheel-ruts that keep you doing the same thing over and over and over again. Remember, the process is always in your hands. It is your choice when and how to use it. It is your choice whether to use the guidance as a directive or a pointer, your choice whether to treat divining as the word of the Absolute, as an understanding friend to hash things through with, or as an adviser with a useful viewpoint. You are the scientific investigator here—running a test on your life, going in a certain direction, getting input, making a decision, and then looking at the results. If this guidance system works for you, keep on going; if not, reevaluate whether it is for you. Go as slow or fast as you choose.

The odds are high that your leap of faith will be rewarded with immediate payoff: ease, clarity, synchronicity. And that, in turn, can lead you to the realization of your true self—the you that is not only part of everything, but *is* everything.

WHERE IS THE ANSWER COMING FROM?

For much of human history, people saw everything in the world as intricately connected, and they used natural events to divine the future and determine courses of action. Patterns such as the passage of clouds across the sky, the falling of leaves, and the swooping and cries of birds held rich personal meaning and conveyed information to them.

Over time, as societies developed, civilizations devised ways to invoke answers rather than merely awaiting them, using bones, shells, sticks, and coins. Religions, especially in the East, used divinatory tools as a way to make contact with the Divine, and often divinatory specialists called oracles or shamans played a central role in important societal and personal decisions.

Divining practices have often been shrouded in rituals, reflecting what is at its heart a deeply mysterious process. How is it that when we ask a question, the answer comes—and it turns out to be remarkably right for our unique situation?

In the most concrete sense, when we divine, the answers are coming from within our body. When we ask a question, brain neurons fire, neurotransmitters flow, electrical currents spark, energy is released into muscle fibers, and something moves to let us know the response on a conscious level—a muscle weakens, a pendulum swings, a chit falls.

What sets this course of physical events in action? Our unconscious, the part of our mind that is "behind the locked door," as *New Yorker* writer Malcolm Gladwell puts it in *Blink: The Power of Thinking Without Thinking*. By definition, it is an area of which we have no active awareness. Scientists can monitor its pathways in the brain with increasingly sophisticated equipment, but they can't pin down where it emanates from: it's like watching the flight pattern of a plane on air-traffic-control radar but not being in the mind of the pilot behind the controls.

The unconscious mind has staggering computing power, scientists have found—it processes eleven million pieces of sensory information at any one moment—and it can effortlessly sort through mountains of data in a split second, frequently with better outcomes for decision-making than the efforts of the conscious mind. It can bring to light things we know but have long forgotten, as well as things we theoretically should not know, such as who is on the other end of the phone before it rings.

The unconscious speaks its mind in our behavior when we find ourselves acting spontaneously, for better or worse, for reasons we can't really explain. It also surfaces in bursts of intuition that are surprisingly spot-on. These intuitive hits often announce themselves through sensations in our body. Gladwell tells of one famous art expert who could detect a fake piece of art because his stomach felt wrong, his ears rang, he felt suddenly depressed, or he felt woozy and off-balance. Depending on our makeup, intuition can be, for instance, a gut feeling, a fleeting mental picture, a word that pops into consciousness, or a sure knowing. When we divine, instead of merely awaiting signals from the unconscious, we invoke them. We ask, and we receive.

So who or what is it that is moving through our unconscious mind to zero in on the answer? For there is a sense of some *thing*, some deep intelligence or wise presence, on the other end of our query.

Some people believe the response is transmitted by an innately intelligent, self-ordering Universe. They feel themselves part of a pulsating web of quantum particles simultaneously linking together everything everywhere. To express this underlying oneness, they may use phrases such as the "Universe," "Pervasive Unity," "Universal Consciousness," or the "web of life." Others talk of the cells of their bodies resonating vibrationally with other forms of life and intelligence, with answers transmitted electromagnetically. Or they view the information as something that emanates from the collective unconscious—as Carl Jung described it, from the memories and wisdom of the entire human race, which shapes our psyche.

Sometimes the "transmitter" feels more personal. Just as waves in the electromagnetic spectrum can translate as vivid colors or X-rays or radio sound, the Divine translates in our consciousness into many forms and layers. Some people feel a strong mental and emotional connection to a specific aspect or personification of the Divine—a wise and loving Being—on which they focus their mind when divining. They may conceive of that energy as God, a higher power, the Absolute, the Highest Universal Energy Source, and for them divining can be a form of prayer, or "putting it in God's hands." Some people, often with an Eastern orientation, feel this from the inside out, saying the answers come from the "God-self within me" or the "part of my self that starts with a capital *S*." Others feel their guidance is coming directly from a great deity, saint, soul, or spiritual teacher, living or not. Or they may feel angels or their guardian angel coming to their aid. Some people speak of getting advice from their spirit guides, who may act singly or collectively and may change depending on the question. Others feel that a departed parent or loved one is speaking to them.

Ultimately, it is all guesswork: the door remains shut, the source unknowable. "The name that can be named is not the eternal Name," advises the *Tao Te Ching*. Some don't even try to figure it out: "How this works, I don't really know," says Bruce Irwin, a professional water dowser in Athol, New York. "You plug in the library card and get information from the great library in the sky."

What is wonderful is that divining doesn't require any particular belief, just an openness to trying it and a willingness to make contact with our innermost self.

Because one thing is clear: we are the vessel through which the wisdom flows. We are the ones who ask the question, who are open to receiving the answer, who give it voice and substance. The answer is within, and divining tools help us to access it. They are hearing aids that turn up the volume of that still, small voice, binoculars that sharpen our inner sight. "This pendulum is nothing in itself, just a piece of metal and plastic," says my friend Kate. "But it's a tool that the higher self uses to help me access my universal knowledge. It teaches me to trust my inner being. When I ask a question and it gives me an answer, I'm not trusting it; I'm trusting myself."

In practice, over time, these tools give us the experience of reality at its most paradoxical: the process seems to be happening simultaneously within us and beyond us, which gives us a taste of what the mystics call ultimate truth. Perhaps Etty Hillesum, whose diaries, *An Interrupted Life,* glow with wisdom, said it most eloquently: "I repose in myself. And that part of myself, that deepest and richest part in which I repose, is what I call 'God.'"

HOW DIVINING CAN BENEFIT YOUR LIFE

Divining is not *the* path; it is *a* path. It may be a path that shapes your life, or it may be a minor one, something that augments your other approaches and comes in handy in a crunch. You may use it once in your life, or once a day. You may find it useful at some points and not others, or with some types of questions and not others.

From one viewpoint, it is a path of surrender. You are surrendering your lower self to your higher self, "my will" to "Divine will." You are putting aside your ego—that stubborn and childish foot-stamper that knows it's right—so that your wiser self, tuned in to a deeper level, can prevail. In this surrender, you are laying down your inner armaments—defenses, judgments, conditioned patterns of resistance. It may feel like you're giving up control, but that's just your ego protesting, as it's wont to do. In fact, paradoxically, the process gives you a sense of more control; it is, after all, you who is consciously posing the question, awaiting the answer, and moving forward with that new information. "Divining is one way of accessing my inner knowing when I'm not feeling connected," says my friend Tessa. "I muscle-test when I'm out of control—when I'm feeling confused. Testing puts me *back* in control."

Whether you use divining as a path, an ancillary practice, or an occasional godsend, it has a host of benefits: it gives you access to deeper wisdom, makes life both efficient and adventurous, helps you sidestep mistakes, calms the mind, enhances synchronicity, accelerates your spiritual progress, and lightens your step. Let's look more closely at these:

It Allows You to Bypass Your Conscious Mind to Access Deeper Wisdom

The conscious mind has its job cut out managing the details of our lives: deciding what it wants, plotting how to get there, overcoming obstacles, making choices, evaluating results, figuring out how to do things better next time. Once in human history this left-brained managing mind was balanced out by our intuitive right brain, but over time it has become very bossy indeed, adamantly overriding all opposition. "It's the mind's job to be right, and it will kill for it," says spiritual teacher Byron Katie.

We are loyal to the conscious mind in spite of the fact that it often does a poor job. Dutch researchers, for example, have found that logically and carefully weighing all the options in a complex decision leads to poorer choices than leaving it to the unconscious mind to sort out, because we aren't very good at anticipating relative benefits and impacts on a rational level. They also discovered that shoppers who carefully think a major purchase through are actually less happy afterward with their choice.[2]

Divining allows you to move past the conscious mind into your more efficient unconscious mind, where you can then—very important—receive communication back. It accomplishes this because its tools actually give the conscious mind something to do so that it can relax and allow our deeper intelligence to run the show. Divining engages the left, analytical side of our brain—the part most associated with conscious thought-processes—to frame the question, interpret the answer, and validate the results. It engages the right side of our brain—the part most associated with unconscious processes—to sink into a state of receptivity and receive the answer in a clear, empty space. This process is described as "thinking narrow, being wide," by Tom Graves, author of *The Diviner's Handbook*, and it has the effect of seamlessly integrating our brain activity. In doing so, it gives the wiser part of our mind a stronger voice. The truth is, we often know deep down what we have to do, but we don't want to admit it because it's too frightening, radical, or counterintuitive. The pendulum, muscle-testing, and chits are concrete tools that give clout to that deeper reality; they can't be ignored as easily as that still, small inner voice.

It Makes Life Efficient

We like to think we have a firm grip on the vagaries of life, but the truth is, almost anything can happen at any time. There is no way to know all of the variables that will affect something that will happen a year from now, a month from now, tomorrow, or even in the next hour. At its heart, decision-making is a guessing game.

Consumer purchases, for example, can take up huge amounts of our mental space, as we figure out what we need, what the comparative advantages are, who sells it, and what we can afford. The more anxious we are about the purchase, the more clouded our mind can be. Take something as simple as buying a multivitamin. There are dozens of products on the shelves with their ingredients listed. But even if we've done our research carefully and know that we want, say, 500 milligrams of vitamin C and 100 milligrams of selenium, we don't necessarily know the current reputation of the manufacturer, the quality of the ingredients, whether there is any contamination, or whether what studies advise is actually what our unique body needs. Divining makes all of this easy as pie. You test each bottle with your fingers or a pendulum and get a clear answer: this product is the best choice. The information is being sorted through for you, saving you time, trouble, and money. When I was packing to go to India for seventeen months, I had so much to do that I had no time to research anything, so I muscle-tested for three multivitamins formulated by physicians I had interviewed for magazine articles; a No came up for each. Puzzled, I muscle-tested my way through the alphabet and came up with the name of another doctor with whom I had little rapport; her website had a multivitamin package that turned out to be perfect because it included fish oil and other components that I had been planning to buy separately.

Another time, out of curiosity, I used a pendulum to check the products in my bathroom and got a strong No for my contact-lens solution. I was puzzled, but changed brands—and a few months later, the media reported that the first brand had contamination problems linked to eye infections that were robbing some people of their sight.

Divining can also save you from wasting energy and money on ventures that don't pan out. Faith Houston of Morris, New York, was excited to learn that a feng shui master was leading a tour to China, but to her disappointment, when she muscle-tested the question, *Should I go on this trip?* she got a No. "It really annoyed me," she recalls. "When an e-mail came a year later about another trip, I expected another No, but to my surprise, I got a Yes." When she called the feng shui master for more information, he told her the last trip had been canceled at the last moment because of a bird-flu outbreak.

It Opens Up Adventurous Possibilities

When you divine, you let go of your death grip on your life. You open yourself up to all options, even the scary ones. This puts you on the razor's edge of growth. It loosens your attachments to making things happen exactly as you want, and this opens up a space in which even more amazing things can unfold. As life coach Sue Freeman of Chester, New Jersey, puts it: "I have learned that there are many possibilities, sometimes ones we can't even imagine, and if we allow for any possibility instead of limiting ourselves, we can be very surprised how much better the opportunities that come our way will be." Divining also demolishes concepts that keep us bound—concepts from our upbringing that may have made sense when we were struggling to figure out the world, but no longer do.

As you develop trust in the process, you'll find that it gives you the courage to take bold steps. Taking a particular trip may seem ruinous financially, but on that trip you may find your next employer or career track. Many times I've had to breathe deeply and move forward, and the answers I've divined have worked out in ways that have left me awed. For example, once I did the chits and was directed to India for four months—when I had a full-time freelance job at a women's magazine that involved producing and writing a weekly photo essay. I couldn't even imagine informing the editor-in-chief that I would be away a third of the year, but immediately I found someone highly qualified who could step in for me temporarily and I was able to figure out ways to preproduce much of my work. The editor laughed, gave me her blessing, and told me she envied me the journey.

It Helps You Sidestep Mistakes

In the larger sense, there are no mistakes, just learning experiences. But speaking logistically rather than philosophically, divining can mean far fewer muddles, detours, and dead ends. It can head off the wrong action before it's too late, as happened with Joe and Marta Smith's December drive from Nebraska to New Mexico to see Joe's dying mother. Sitting down to lunch at their farm, they used a pendulum to ask if they should leave in one day or two. No, it advised, leave immediately. They did and were safely out of the state by the time an unexpectedly severe ice storm blew in that night. They were by his mother's side when she died. Coming back later with a U-Haul, they used a pendulum to find roads clear of ice, snow, and wrecks. They ended up zigzagging their way home on highways they normally wouldn't have taken, and avoided another major storm.

As you get better with your divining practice, you can hone in on technical information that you would otherwise have no way of knowing. When Faith Houston moved into an old Victorian house, she hired an architect to design a new fireplace to replace the original, which had been removed. But she got an uneasy feeling looking at the plans. She promptly muscle-tested: *Is this the most appropriate design for this room?* No. She began sorting through the options—aesthetics, finances, specifications—and finally what came up was that one structural element was too small by an inch and a half. The architect redesigned it. "You walk in that room now and you wouldn't know that fireplace hadn't been there forever. It fits perfectly," she said later.

Divining can also help us navigate past certain weak spots in our psyches that tend to lead us into rough waters. The area in which I have usually had trouble separating fantasy from reality is relationships. Once, I was thoroughly tempted to get involved with a tall, sweet, Paul Newman look-alike. I asked the chits, and got a clear answer: forget it. So I did, and it turned out, as time went on, that we had our differences. A year later, he met one of my best friends, married her, and they're deliriously happy. Good advice!

It Calms the Mind by Stopping Dithering, Second-Guessing, and Regrets

Carolyn Touryniere's bike was stolen in Key West. She wanted to buy another one, but every time she pendled for it, she was advised not to. Instead, the pendulum said, Take the bus, and it hinted at a relationship. Reluctantly, she followed the advice. After about a week, the bus driver asked her out. Their romance lasted only about five weeks, but it turned out to be an important relationship for her.

Soon after it broke off, she found her bike again—in a pawn shop, so there had been no need for her to buy a new one. "Divining adds an element of surprise and delight to life because it takes you down a path you wouldn't ordinarily go," she says.

When, like Carolyn, we have a choice to make, it can get very noisy in the mind: Should I, shouldn't I, what if this or that, how will it happen, what will they say, how much will it cost, what if this problem comes up . . . and on and on. Just going back and forth mentally can prolong decision-making for weeks or months, or even longer; in fact, the more choices we have, the less likely we are to make a decision at all, psychologists have found. Because this to-and-fro keeps the mind restlessly engaged, it also blots out the deeper silence that opens up into true happiness and the experience of our true nature.

Divining stops this process cold. The choices are in front of you, and one is selected. Period, full stop. Your mind at that point swings into another mode: watching what unfolds with the choice. Second-guessing is short-circuited because you know—through experience, over time—that it always turns out for the best. Buyer's remorse—a process so reliable that sales people are taught ways to ward it off—becomes a thing of the past.

It also teaches you to love what is, to accept what is unfolding without unnecessary anguish or misery. Because you experience being taken care of, you're at peace with what comes up and you learn to adjust to it, which means you don't go through life kicking and screaming at turns of events. You also don't blame yourself; you have more trust that whatever you're going through is for your own greater good.

Divining doesn't eliminate worry, sorrow, or anger, and it doesn't mean you bypass illness, financial stress, loss, and death. Nothing on the planet can do that. But because you feel embedded in the Divine, you can deal with hard times more easily. By putting you in tune with the underlying pattern of the Universe, divining gives you a broader viewpoint. You trust that your difficulties have somehow a higher purpose and a limited life span and that, in some way, grace or clarity will come out of it. Help is just an inner query away, and you get what you need, day by day, step-by-step.

It Invites Synchronicity and Enhances Flow

Synchronicity—meaningful coincidence—is a word coined by Jung. It is the coming together of an inner thought with an outer event in a way that has an emotional or psychological impact on us and gives us a sense of being part of a larger whole. Jung believed that synchronicity demonstrates the dynamic interrelationship between our consciousness and the outer world, and that it is as important in explaining the workings of the Universe as cause and effect. For example, let's say you think for the first time in years of a high school classmate and run into him on the street a few hours later: that's synchronicity. It's even more amazing if you learn that he's working for a company that you want to get a job with—and he tells you that a co-worker is quitting in a few days, so there will be an opening. When synchronicities like that happen one after another, like popcorn popping in a pan, we're in flow, which is the natural, effortless unfolding of our lives in a way that moves us toward wholeness and harmony. When we are in flow, occurrences line up, events fall into place, and obstacles melt away. Rather than life being a meaningless struggle, it is permeated with a deep sense of purposefulness and order.

Divining puts you in the right place at the right time so that synchronicity can unfold in its eye-popping way, and flow becomes a given in your life. In fact, this is one of the great delights of divining, and ultimate proof that it works. I experienced that with my four-month trip to India. Using the chits, I got information to leave New York on March 7 and return on July 3. On my third day in India, I got a phone call—literally the only point on that trip in which I was reachable. My father, who had been diagnosed with Lou Gehrig's disease at Christmas, had taken a sudden turn for the worse and could die at any moment. I took a plane straight home to Indianapolis, where my sisters and brothers had gathered. He decided to turn off his respirator, but when he started gasping for breath, he yielded to our pleas and agreed to go back on it. Because I was totally free from job, housing, and social obligations, I was able to spend a month helping my stepmother find a good nursing home for him and getting him established there.

Then, following the chits again, I returned to India. My good friend Charlene Belitz joined me, and a number of incredible chit-driven events unfolded that took us to Tibet and Nepal, which would eventually lead to us co-authoring *The Power of Flow: Practical Ways to Transform Your Life with Meaningful Coincidence.*

My father, meanwhile, decided to end his life by going off the respirator. He had no joy in his days; bed-bound, he couldn't speak, had to have his lungs suctioned out every few hours, and could no longer enjoy golf or scotch. He chose July 6, because on that date Medicaid stopped picking up the respirator expenses of $35,000 a month, and he wanted that money to go to us children rather than the nursing home. The decision brought him out of his depression and gave him a sense of control and purpose. I returned in time to spend the last two days with him, and I was with him as he left his body. It was a sacred and beautiful moment, and I had a sense of wild ecstasy, as though sharing his delight at being unshackled.

The divined dates had proven themselves providential, and they were also key in events that unfolded in Charlene's life. Because we took a certain flight out of Tibet to get me back home on time, she helped calm a Tibetan passenger having a severe panic attack. Charlene stayed with his family in Kathmandu for a month and brought back to the States his twenty-two-year-old sister. The hard-to-get visa was approved because Charlene established a rapport with the U.S. embassy official in Kathmandu, who had once taught at the same Denver university where Charlene was teaching. A year later, in New York, the young woman met and married a nephew of the Dalai Lama, fulfilling a prophetic dream she had had as a child that she would meet her Tibetan husband in the United States.

This story isn't that unique. You'll find that as you grow in trust with divining, you'll get a sense of skipping through life hand in hand with the Universe.

It Accelerates Growth on Your Spiritual Path

When we divine and get an answer out of the blue, so to speak, we experience the Universe as responsive. It cares. This can be a shock at first—we're not alone in the world, after all—and it often puts us on a path that is consciously spiritual. We're now open to other help that comes our way—teachers, classes, books, yoga, meditation—and as our sense of spirituality widens with time, we soon come to see that there is nothing in our life that is not a spiritual teacher. In the meantime, divining can play that role: gently directing us down certain paths, rewarding courage, developing our discrimination, and most importantly, teaching us trust—trust in ourselves and the unfolding of our destiny. Like a good teacher, it challenges us, but reassures us. It is tuned into our exact needs.

Those needs most likely include some, shall we say, inner housecleaning. "It can bring your karma thumping in, in a big hurry," says Leroy Bull of the American Society of Dowsers. The adverse beliefs and stubborn behaviors that block us from being all we can be will inevitably surface during the course of our divining, just as they surface in our daily interactions with others. Divining will make them clear as a bell and direct us on our healing journey. "If you have an issue with a certain thing, testing will keep you circling around it until you're clear it's an issue, and then you can work on it," says kinesiology teacher Darlene Van de Grift. "The answers you receive are not necessarily right per se, but right for your process—they give you the answers you need to accelerate your growth. They align you to your life purpose."

To guide you along that path, an answer can be a stepping-stone rather than a final step. That was what Sue Freeman experienced when, unhappy in her marriage, she repeatedly consulted the pendulum. Yes, get a divorce, it advised. She saw a lawyer, put down a retainer, and informed her husband. "I had a certain vision in my mind of his being angry or not caring, but in actuality, I found out just how much he loves me—and finally, after years of asking him to go to marriage counseling, he agreed," she says. "The answer Yes turned out to be good. By following it, I changed things in our relationship where in the past I was not able to. It turned out even better than I could possibly have imagined."

Sometimes, in fact, divining will push us deeper into a painful pattern—for our ultimate good, if not for our immediate comfort. By keeping us pinned to our process—if we so wish!—divining ultimately takes us down a spiritual path that improves our clarity and opens our heart. Maybe that is why it's not known to be that successful at making us rich overnight by supplying us with, say, a winning lottery number or horse-race winner, and it may not whisk us into film stardom either. "If you want to be rich and famous, divining might take you as far as you need to go to meet the people you need to meet so that you lose that desire," says kinesiology counselor Barbara Lubow. "That is, unless you're meant to be rich and famous—for some people, that's their job."

It Lightens Life
To be honest, what's more interesting than our own life? We naturally love talking about ourselves, and divining is a way to do that with a very receptive listener, especially if we dialogue with it. Divining is interactive and playful, and it adds intrigue and delight to decision-making processes that would otherwise be boring, drab, or stressful. "There's an element of fun in divining that brightens the dullness of everyday consciousness," says Garnette Arledge, author of *Wise Secrets of Aloha* and *On Angel's Eve.* "When I was a teenager, I would pray, 'Please, I don't want to live a dull, normal life,' and it ensures that I don't!"

By throwing our fate to the winds, which is what divining feels like sometimes, we can feel as free as the clouds floating by. Instead of the heaviness of having to get it right, we experience a lighthearted willingness to dive into the currents of life. That keeps us from taking ourselves too seriously—nonattachment that is a great spiritual boon. Sitting in the palm of the Divine, we can relax and enjoy the view.

YOU CAN USE DIVINING WHEN . . .

You're in a Pinch

When we're in a genuine dilemma and we don't trust our gut or have a clear answer within, divining works exceptionally well. Our need seems to empower the process, and as long as we disengage our emotions from it or use a technique like the chits that emotions can't override, the answer will come swiftly, with a sense of rightness and inevitability to it.

You Need a Friend with Whom to Talk Things Over

With muscle-testing and the pendulum, you can actually talk an issue through, exploring all the options, testing possible outcomes, going down new avenues of thought as you probe the possibilities. The more honest you are with yourself, the more useful the answers will be.

You Need a Reality Check

We can get so enmeshed in our mental patterns, desires, and projections that we can't see something clearly, which is why we do things like marry the same person over and over, only in different bodies. Divining can give us the straight story.

You Need a Dose of Courage

Divining has a way of taking us down roads we fear to tread. We often know deep down what has to be done, and divining prods us by lending authority to that knowing. Then we find that our fears were exaggerated, groundless, or worth going through.

You Have to Sort Through Information
To find the right plumber, jacket, mattress, or mutual fund, all you need is a list and a divining tool. Just be sure to define your terms clearly. You can also expand the simple Yes/No protocol to efficiently pinpoint numbers, quantities, and dates—for example, to choose the best day and time to travel.

CHAPTER 2

LAMAS, SOLDIERS, PHYSICISTS

THE HISTORY AND EVOLVING THEORY OF DIVINING

Lhasa, Tibet, March 1959. A final, fatal confrontation was in the air between the Chinese troops grouping just outside the city and tens of thousands of distraught Tibetans who had surrounded the Dalai Lama's summer palace to prevent his being arrested by the Chinese. Inside, the twenty-four-year-old Dalai Lama again called in his official medium, the Nechung Oracle, who had twice that week counseled him to stay put. In his autobiography, Freedom in Exile, *the Dalai Lama writes: "To my astonishment, he shouted, 'Go! Go! Tonight!' The medium, still in his trance, then staggered forward and, snatching up some paper and a pen, wrote down, quite clearly and explicitly, the route that I should take out of the Norbulingka, down to the last Tibetan town on the Indian border." The Dalai Lama double-checked the counsel using Mo, a divining system akin to casting lots, and it concurred. Against all odds, under the noses of vast numbers of Chinese troops, the Dalai Lama succeeded in escaping Tibet on horseback that night.*

ACROSS CULTURES AND CONTINENTS

When we're in a dilemma and turn to divining, we're in good company. "All peoples during all historical periods have practiced divination as a way of exploring the unknown, solving problems, diagnosing ailments, and prescribing medicines and other healing treatments," writes divination scholar Barbara Tedlock, PhD, of the State University of New York at Buffalo, author of *The Woman in the Shaman's Body.*[1]

Originally, people looked for signs in the natural world that appeared out of the blue, so to speak: crows flying to the left or right, clouds forming certain shapes, the first spring flower to blossom, the first animal to cross their path on the first day of the year. This has its limitations. As Ray Grasse points out in *The Waking Dream: Unlocking the Symbolic Language of Our Lives:* "Though useful when they happen, one can never be sure when an omen might take place. One can't very well wait for a comet to blaze through the sky or an animal to appear at one's window before making an important decision. Consequently, humans have developed an assortment of methods to induce omenological messages at will. Given the order and harmony seen as underlying all events, it was believed that the inherent meaningfulness of the universe could be tapped whenever desired to answer specific questions."

Across cultures and continents, people have successfully used sticks, stones, mirrors, knives, kites, ponds, mandalas, books, betel nuts, cards, tea leaves, animals, numbers, stars, shells—anything at hand—to pluck information out of the environment. Scholars have identified at least seventy categories of divination, many of which fall into the following three approaches (detailed in later chapters):

1. Casting of lots. The random throwing or tossing of objects, seeing where they land, and interpreting the results to obtain an answer to a question. Perhaps the oldest form of divining, it was used in ancient Assyria with pebbles, in Greece and Rome with sheep knucklebones, in China with yarrow stalks and the *I Ching*, in Norseland with runes. Today, it's used in tossing a coin to settle a dispute, in throwing dice, and in lotteries, which involve the random selection of a number or name.

2. Dowsing. Using a tool to amplify intuition and access information beyond the five senses. Y-shaped twigs and rods have been used to locate water and metals in societies ranging from ancient Egypt through eighteenth-century Germany to present-day rural Oklahoma. The pendulum, a weight hanging from a string or chain, has been used in virtually every society. For example, the Cherokee have used it to locate lost articles, the Finnish and Russians to detect sources of disease in the body, and Australian, British, and Italian soldiers to locate water sources in enemy territory. According to the *Observer,* a military newspaper, U.S. Marines in Vietnam successfully used wire coat-hangers to dowse for Vietcong tunnels and underground bunkers.[2]

3. Kinesthetic. Using one's body as the instrument of insight. As societies developed, this often became the province of trained experts called oracles or shamans, who predicted events and prescribed actions, often through the portal of an altered state induced by music, fasting, chanting, or hallucinogens. Oracles played key roles in Egyptian, Greek, Indian, and Nigerian societies, among others. Shamanism, the religion of indigenous peoples, revolves around mediums skillful at communicating with other dimensions of existence to solve problems.

DIVINING AS A RELIGIOUS PRACTICE

In many religions, divining has played a role, particularly in Eastern philosophies that stress the interconnectedness of all things. The *I Ching*, or *Book of Changes*, is a divinatory text that is the bible of Confucianism. People toss yarrow stalks or coins to divine a pattern, then consult the *I Ching* to understand the larger context in which events are unfolding and to get specific advice on whether to advance, retreat, or remain still. (Scholars speculate that the orderly worldview, flexibility, and respect for authority embedded in that text do much to account for the success of capitalism in Confucian-based societies in China, Japan, and South Korea.)

Perhaps no religious tradition has developed a more profound understanding of the intricacies and foibles of the human mind than Tibetan Buddhism. Its teachings explore the most subtle levels of cognition in a way that makes Western psychology look rudimentary. When its most advanced practitioners make a major decision, divining systems are used to bypass the logical mind to access deeper wisdom.

The Dalai Lama, a learned sage of the highest order, regularly consults the Nechung Oracle, a monk who enters a trance state in which his body is believed to be possessed by an entity that supplies information from subtle spiritual realms. High lamas routinely use a system of divination called Mo, which is a casting of lots. It is still performed in monasteries under secretive conditions, but—this being the time of the Tibetan diaspora and the diffusion of its wisdom—you can also purchase a book on Mo over the Internet. A Buddhist nun who was part of the entourage of a famous Tibetan lama once told me that they would arrange for him to speak in, say, Singapore, and the night before leaving, he would toss some small objects and decide to go, not go, change the date, or send someone else instead.

In Hinduism, astrology, which is a formalized system of divination, is used to determine whether marriage partners are compatible, raising the chances of happiness in arranged marriages.

In Western religions, some researchers believe that when the Torah or Old Testament speaks of Urim and Thummim, two stones in the breastplate given to Moses on Mount Sinai and used by a succession of high priests, it is speaking of divining tools, Urim representing Yes and Thummim being No. In the New Testament, the apostle Matthias was chosen to replace Judas by a casting of lots. Although divining is frowned upon in some Christian churches today, Christians will sometimes ask a question, pray, and open the Bible at random for an answer, a divining method known as bibliomancy.

THE SHIFTING SCIENTIFIC WORLDVIEW

Elizabeth Lloyd Mayer, a psychology professor and researcher at the University of California at Berkeley, felt her world of rationality crumble when her eleven-year-old daughter's prized and rare harp was stolen after a concert in Oakland. After trying every avenue to find it, in desperation Mayer followed the advice of a friend and sought the help of a dowser. The president of the American Society of Dowsers, Harold McCoy, asked her to mail him a map of Oakland; he scanned it using a pendulum, and then called to tell her the exact house the harp was in. The police refused to act, so she plastered posters within a two-block radius of the house, offering a reward for the harp. Furtive phone calls came in, and a few days later, in a dark parking lot, she was handed the instrument.

The episode caused her months of sleepless nights; no part of her belief system could explain how a man sitting in a trailer in Arkansas could locate a stolen harp in Oakland. She embarked on a decade-long exploration and found "a vast, strange new territory of research regarding . . . interactions between mind and matter that simply cannot be contained inside what we call normal science," as she described it in *Extraordinary Knowing: Science, Skepticism, and the Inexplicable Powers of the Human Mind.*

Her initial skepticism was typical: science has, naturally enough, had a hard time with the unseen aspects of divining. This persists in spite of the fact that cutting-edge studies by quantum physicists, neuroscientists, and cell biologists are dismantling cause-and-effect explanations of physical reality. "One of the hallmarks of much late twentieth- and early twenty-first-century science has been its failure to conform to mental images drawn from our everyday experience. Instead, scientists are now imagining parallel universes, quantum nonlocality, wormholes in time and space, mass-energy transformations, cosmic strings, gravity-bent light and other strange concepts that defy common-sense reality," writes Tedlock. As one physicist put it, quantum reality is not only stranger than we think, it's stranger than we *can* think.

Quantum physics has revealed that we live in—and are—a vast ocean of pulsating energy that is 99.999999% empty space. The teacup in your hand, even your hand itself, is not solid matter but actually particles and waveforms of energy that are connected in nearly unfathomable ways to everything else in the universe.

The breeze on our face, the twinge in our back, the look in our lover's eyes: physicist David Bohm speculated that these "realities" that we perceive within ourselves and without emerge in each moment from a shapeless, infinite void of pure potentiality. The universe is one of "unbroken wholeness," he writes, with information being transmitted and received everywhere all at once.[3] Indeed, in exploring the zero-point field, the so-called empty space between quantum particles, scientists are finding a heaving sea of flux that seems to dynamically link all things in ways that boggle the mind. The effects are nonlocal, which is to say, space and time don't matter. In hundreds of tightly controlled trials at the Stanford Research Institute and the Princeton Engineering Anomalies Research lab, ordinary people were asked to mentally focus their attention on a person at an unknown location; about two-thirds of the time, they did better than chance at describing what he was seeing around him, such as shoppers in a mall or a boat arena. Often they were able to describe the scene *ahead* of the time he arrived there, hours before he himself knew of the site.[4] The scientists found that almost all of us, if we're relaxed and feeling playful, can do this kind of thing and get better at it with practice; it's just that we typically don't ask it of ourselves.

What does this suggest for divining? Unfathomable amounts of information are available to us, if we're relaxed and open enough to tap into it. When we ask a question, our thoughts may produce a subtle, specific vibration that catapults through time and space to resonate with the target with that same vibration. It's like tuning in to a radio station: when we fix the dial on a target, the radio's receivers instantly connect with that frequency out of thousands of choices to pull in the music we want. The attitude we take and the skills we develop—which involve putting aside preconceptions, emotions, and desires— enable the signal to come through clear and strong.

THE DOWNSIDE OF OVERTHINKING

Some scientists speculate that the unconscious—the part of our mind from which concepts emerge, seemingly out of nowhere—may interact easily with the zero-point field, the flux between particles from which physical reality emerges, seemingly out of nowhere. Some wonder, in fact, if they are not one and the same thing. Our unconscious, as personal as it feels, may emanate not from the gray matter of our brain but from a vast, pulsating universe of potentiality that is simultaneously inside and outside our bodies.

The unconscious, scientists have found, seems to have unfathomable abilities; it is like a parallel supercomputer compared to the cumbersome adding machine that is our conscious mind. It can process vast quantities of information in a split second and spit out an answer, as long as the conscious mind doesn't meddle too much. In *Blink,* Malcolm Gladwell writes of "thin-slicing," the ability of our unconscious to find patterns in situations and behavior based on very narrow slices of experience. He tells of marriage researchers who can tell in an hour if a marriage will be intact in fifteen years, and a tennis coach who can forecast a double fault before a serve is completed. In part, it's because they've built up a dense body of knowledge about a subject, and in part, it's because they trust their gut. We all have that instinctive knack of sorting through information without conscious thought, it seems. For example, students watching a two-second silent video clip of a professor gave the same rating of effectiveness as students who had the professor for a full semester. But the information is not infallible, Gladwell points out; it can come through distorted if we are blind-sided by erroneous prejudgments, such as racial stereo-typing, or if we are disabled by strong emotions such as fear or anger—factors that also lead divining astray.

Relying on the conscious mind can actually be coun-terproductive when making a complicated decision, Dutch scientists have found. In one of many such experiments, when people were asked to choose between four cars distinguished by twelve variables, such as gas efficiency, legroom, and stereo systems, those thinking it through carefully and conscientiously made the best choice 23% of the time; people whose unconscious mind did the work (because they were distracted with puzzles) chose cor-rectly 60% of the time. The conscious mind, said study leader Ap Dijksterhuis at the University of Amsterdam, can process only a limited amount of information at once and isn't good at weighing the relative importance of many factors, whereas the unconscious is better at integrating large amounts of information. His research also found that thinking a lot about a complicated purchase like furniture or a sound system makes us actually more prone to buyer's remorse afterward. On the other hand, we're likely to be more satisfied with a consciously-made purchase if we're buying a simple item with few factors to weigh, like an umbrella or paper towels.[5]

The best strategy, it seems, is not to prize one mode over the other, but to allow both the conscious mind and the unconscious mind a voice. In our culture, attaining that balance usually means giving the unconscious its due and its say. Divining is an approach that provides the tools for that, and because it accesses both modes—conscious and unconscious, left brain and right brain—it can help us to deftly sort out the real from the unreal, the superior from the inferior.

THE MYSTERY OF FREE WILL DEEPENS

As a society, we prize rational decision-making, yet the more deeply neuroscientists examine conscious choice, the less logical and more mysterious it looks. German researchers, in a study published in *Nature Neuroscience,* reported that the brain appears to make up its mind ten seconds before we consciously decide to do something. Asked to push buttons with their left or right hand at random and at their own pace, subjects wired to MRIs showed brain activity ten seconds before they made a conscious decision to press a particular button; 70% of the time, scientists could predict in advance which button they would push.[6] "We think our decisions are conscious, but these data show that consciousness is just the tip of the iceberg. This doesn't rule out free will, but it does make it implausible," study head John-Dylan Haynes of the Bernstein Center for Computational Neuroscience in Berlin told the *Wall Street Journal.*[7] The study seems to back up the words of spiritual teacher Eckhart Tolle in *A New Earth:* "'I think' is just as false a statement as 'I digest' or 'I circulate my blood.' Digestion happens, circulation happens, thinking happens."

This is almost too mind-boggling to take in—the conscious mind rebels!—and for many centuries, people have vigorously debated whether or not we have free will. But clearly, we *feel* as if we have it, and flexing the muscle of self-determination is one of the delights of being human. Perhaps with the interactive process of divining, we are experiencing both sides of the coin. When we ask the question, we are enjoying the exercise of our will-power; when we absorb the answer in a receptive state, we are—if just for a moment—enjoying the no-effort state of "being willed."

RIGHT BRAIN *AND* LEFT BRAIN

Like much of cutting-edge science, studies on divining raise more questions than they answer. Scientists typically focus on water dowsing, since the results are easily verifiable. For example, a rigorous ten-year German peer-reviewed study found that drill teams directed by dowsers had a success rate of 96% in finding water in an arid region of Sri Lanka, far above the 30–50% rate of conventional drilling methods.[8] But when scientists bring dowsing out of the field and into a laboratory—surprise! All bets are off. "Whenever someone's tried to do a scientific study, whatever makes dowsing work has either sulked and refused to play at all in the laboratory (though continued to work quite happily outside), or followed the experimenter's theory for a while and then suddenly changed its mind, and worked some other way instead. Awkward as ever!" writes Tom Graves in *The Dowser's Workbook*. Luckily for us—and for pandas, who can't breed easily in a lab but manage it just fine in nature—laboratory findings are not the final word but a work in progress.

There is another way to study divining. Using sophisticated equipment, neuroscientists can peer inside the circuitry of the brain to see what is "lighting up," and brain studies of dowsers, although very preliminary, are highly intriguing; they show a unique pattern of brain-wave activity that differs from that of skilled meditators. When a dozen experienced dowsers were wired up to EEG machines and told to dowse with a pendulum for water sources underneath the building, activity simultaneously occurred in all four brain-wave frequencies: beta waves (ordinary waking consciousness, the busy, buzzing mind), alpha waves (calm, relaxed, peaceful), theta waves (between wakefulness and sleep, as well as dreaming), and delta waves (deep, dreamless sleep; also seen during intense spiritual and psychic experiences). In effect, they were thinking, relaxing, dozing, and sleeping deeply, all at the same time.[9] This extraordinary pattern is "something that apparently not even the accomplished yogi can exhibit when he performs his *siddhis* or paranormal wonders," write T. Edward Ross and Richard D. Wright in *The Divining Mind*. Furthermore, the neurons were firing simultaneously on both sides of the brain, in an even and coherent manner, indicating a synchronization that amplifies the brain's power.

These dowsers were highly skilled, and most likely developed these patterns with practice over time, just as meditators do. In fact, they typically showed that pattern, although less markedly, even when they weren't dowsing, which could indicate that dowsing helps mold the brain over the years.

The study makes sense to Joe Smith, a retired farmer and long-term dowser, who can carry on an animated conversation while still dropping into the theta state typical of someone on the edge of sleep. "It's like controlling the pulse of your heart by clearing your mind," he says. "I can drop my pulse to 38 or 40—they run and get another nurse!" The more he dowses, he says, "the more I seem to be in the right temperament of mind for it."

The findings dovetail with the anthropological research of Tedlock. Because science has often relegated divining to the realm of the irrational, it might be speculated that divining activity takes place in the intuitive, nonlinear part of the brain. But in her examination of studies of diviners in Africa, Latin America, and North America, Tedlock found that diviners use both sides of their brain. For example, they intuitively take in images and symbols, sort through them in an orderly way, interpret them, and then discuss with the client the cause of the problem and how to respond—tasks that indicate not just brain activity in the left and right lobes, but the coursing of neurons across the fiber passageways between the two sides called the corpus callosum, indicating that they are integrating both modalities.[10]

Really good dowsers seem to be in a relaxed but alert state throughout the divining process, able to move limberly and seamlessly from task to task and mode to mode. This is a process that you too will experience as you work with the tools in this book. When you ask a question of a divining system, you use your analytical left brain to frame the question precisely, your intuitive right brain to settle into a state of receptivity to pose the question and receive the answer, and your left brain to evaluate it and decide on the next question or step, which may be supplied intuitively.

As you get better at it over time, you'll feel yourself moving in a delicate dance of opposites: you'll be relaxed yet alert, neutral yet engaged, surrendered yet fully participating. Interestingly, this is also the paradoxical state in which spiritual insights blossom, and changes in consciousness manifest. In *An Experience of Enlightenment,* Flora Courtois describes the "linchpin of enlightenment" as a state akin to sitting deeply relaxed in a silent forest, waiting with intense alertness for ultimate danger that can strike at any moment from any direction. "Attention telescopes to point zero at the center and simultaneously opens to infinity at the periphery. Yet neither center nor periphery remains," she writes.

People in highly evolved states of consciousness often report experiencing a luminous spaciousness that pervades all matter, and sometimes longtime dowsers report a similar sensation. "The longer you're at dowsing, the quieter you become and the more it becomes a clear, empty space on which things are written," says Leroy Bull.

Divining, indeed, can lead us to higher, expanded states of consciousness. It must, because we are fully engaging with the Divine and experiencing sacred energies in a relaxed yet purposeful manner. As we sit receptively awaiting a response, our mind becomes still, and in that moment, we touch the Ineffable.

CHAPTER 3

CUSTOMIZED BY YOU

DESIGNING YOUR OWN
PLAY OF CONSCIOUSNESS

Quantum physicists and mystics increasingly agree: what we believe shapes our personal reality. The outer world we experience mirrors our inner world. In practical terms, this means that with our beliefs and mental patterns, we continually create and re-create our own life drama. Our consciousness crafts our experience.

Divining is no exception: it is our own personal play of consciousness. However we design it, it works. Whatever rules we set up, it responds to.

It is highly useful, though, to learn divining systematically because by doing that, we stand on the shoulders of the many people who have divined before us. We don't have to figure it all out from scratch; they have found what works most powerfully and effectively.

Before you plunge into the actual techniques of the tools, there are five preliminary things to consider that will help you shape your divining processes. They are: determining when you will use it, deciding when and how you will follow its counsel, understanding how it differs from manifesting, taking into account its accuracy, and learning to trust it.

For You to Determine: When Will You Use It?

The whole gamut of options is available to you. Some people report using only one tool once in a great while; for instance, they might use the pendulum on occasion to check what foods on their shelves are good for them, or they might use the chits to ask if they should move to a new town. Other people say they use a particular tool all the time; in a single day, they might muscle-test for the best route to work, which doctor to see, what entrée to order at lunch, when to schedule a business appointment, and so on. Some people divine only when they are truly stuck and don't know what to do; others divine to verify what they already know; others divine on almost everything. There is no right or wrong approach. What matters is what works for you.

The occasions you choose and the frequency also depend on your learning curve. In the beginning, people almost always overuse divining, but that has a practical benefit because you are practicing a skill until it becomes smooth and easy. With time, its use may either increase—especially if you use it to dialogue with yourself about your inner processes—or it may decrease, as intuitive hits show up on their own, unsummoned by tools.

With practice, you'll also develop a pattern that works for you. You may find that it becomes part of your decision-making repertoire, and that you integrate its use with intuition, research, and asking advice of others. Marissa's twelve-year-old car was starting to fail, but whenever she muscle-tested, the answer came back that it wasn't yet time to buy a new one. She muscle-tested before each long trip to make sure she would not have mechanical problems, and always got a go-ahead. One day, she ignored her testing and went to a dealership. The salesman with whom she had an appointment was occupied with another customer for thirty minutes, and when a second salesman spent fifteen minutes unsuccessfully looking for the keys to the only small car on the lot, she left. "I figured the scene was a message from the Universe," she says. A few months later, she woke up in the morning and simply took action. "It didn't occur to me to muscle-test—I just knew it was time," she says. She made a phone call, got the promise of a loan, and within an hour was sitting in a Toyota dealership, talking with a low-key salesman with whom she felt comfortable. She decided on the small, gas-efficient Scion. Back home, she muscle-tested, asking, *Is the car that I saw today the car I should buy? Is that the best buy considering who I am and the money I have available to me?* She got a Yes, but in the next few days, her friends tried to steer her toward a larger car. She kept muscle-testing and kept getting affirmed, but also researched her friends' suggestions on the Internet and found that they were more than she could afford. She went ahead with her purchase, which has proven wise with time: she loves her perky little car and it serves her well. By combining muscle-testing with intuition and research, she was able to move through the process of that major and rather intimidating purchase quickly, smoothly, and with minimal angst.

Sandi and Tom Ruelke of Littleton, New Hampshire, deftly mix pendling with other modes of knowing. Sandi was perusing realty websites when she saw a photo of a ranch house on hilly ground, not the cape on flat land she and Tom had envisioned. "When it came up, the penny dropped. The intuitive knowledge was there: this was the house," she says. They pendled the question, *Should we look at this house?* and got a Yes. They walked through it, liked it, and pendled, *Is this the house for us?* Yes. *What price should we offer?* Asking for a Yes/No answer on different dollar amounts, they got a figure. Says Sandi, "At that point, because it was so important, we called in a backup, a friend of ours who is a good dowser. He confirmed what we had found." They made an offer, and got turned down. That surprised them, but when the realtor suggested they make a counteroffer, they had a gut feeling to say no. They kept looking without success, but gained a greater understanding of the market. Meanwhile, the owners got two more offers, even lower than theirs. After six months, the Ruelkes pendled again for a price and raised their offer, but not by much, and blind-checked it again with another dowser. This time, the owner said yes. "He had an idea of what his house was worth and it took several people making what he thought were ridiculous offers for him to wake up," says Tom. "Because of dowsing, we felt confident waiting it out." They've been there four years, very happily.

For You to Decide: How Much Will You Follow Its Counsel?

From the very first time you divine, you face a key question: how seriously will you take the guidance? The answer to this will determine how far you will let divining take you.

My personal experience is that the more seriously you take it and follow its counsel, the more accurate your results are and the deeper you can go. It makes sense: think of how you feel when someone asks your advice. If it's someone who holds you in high esteem and will do whatever you advise them, you are very careful to give them the wisest advice you can. But if they don't usually take your advice, you're more likely to be flippant. So the more respectful you are when asking a question and the more serious you are about following the counsel, the higher the quality of the information you receive. Earnestness is what is important. It can take nerves of steel, but if your ground rule is that you will follow the counsel, you raise the stakes—and the rewards.

In my divining, I have virtually always followed the advice received from the chits, because they are not easily influenced by emotions. I have generally followed the advice from muscle-testing and the pendulum, but because these are more fluid forms and prone to mental and emotional meddling, I check them more thoroughly and ignore answers that seem off base.

Some people use divining for a second opinion. Rick Jarow, a religious studies professor at Vassar College and author of *Alchemy of Abundance,* says, "It's like you're the CEO and it's the advisory board—you don't have to take its advice because it's not necessarily foolproof, but it's a way of getting a different perspective on the situation." Some use divining like a wise, chatty friend, to talk things through with. "I mix testing with my own thinking, to stretch the possibilities—I'm not absolute about the advice unless it's a matter of life and death," says dancer and counselor Kathleen Donovan.

When you're assessing an answer, it's always important to see if deep down, something clicks that lets you know you're on the right track. Especially for a major life-changing decision, you need that intuitive Yes!—and it is also wise to double-check the counsel, perhaps with another divining approach, and to back it up with deep thinking, research, and talking with wise family and friends, as well as seeing if events unfold to move you in that direction.

On the other hand, if it's not a serious matter, following the advice can have training value for you. "I have, on many occasions, purposely followed through on answers that made no sense at all to me, just to see if the testing was accurate," says Machaelle Small Wright, a renowned muscle-testing teacher. "Doing this and looking at the results with a critical eye is the only way I know to learn about ourselves as kinesiology testers and to discover the nuances and uses of kinesiology itself."

The choice is always yours; it's your life to run. You might want to try an experiment: follow the advice and see what happens; don't follow the advice and see what happens.

Sometimes, after years of divining, people will deliberately not follow the counsel, because life has become so smooth and easy they want a little shaking up. Other times, it might be your destiny to learn a life lesson; divining will improve your clarity, but you'll still go ahead stubbornly, never mind the guidance. "There are times when you won't follow the guidance because it's human nature to rebel," says Darlene Van de Grift. She decided to open a vegan juice bar in spite of not getting the go-ahead with divining. "It clearly said there would be two years of stress, but I was on a roll and wanted to do it, so it didn't matter," she says. "I tested every day several times a day and still got the same answer. Eventually, at some point, I couldn't get an answer—why should it bother answering if I was going to do it anyway? I knew I would be eating crow later, but still, I wanted to be creative and expand in this way." Sure enough, the store did a belly flop and, as she anticipated, she won valuable knowledge from jumping into those waters.

For You to Ponder: How Divining Relates to Manifesting
Many people turn to the tools of manifestation to reach their goals, as popularized in the best-selling book *The Secret*. Although it can be fun and effective, manifesting differs from divining in its basic orientation. Both approaches require intention—mental focus and attunement to the Divine—but manifesting is directive, whereas divining is receptive. Manifesting involves picturing a specific outcome and marshaling our willpower, thoughts, and emotions to nudge it into reality. Divining involves putting aside strong emotions and desires to open ourselves to guidance that meets our deepest needs and highest good, in whatever form that takes. As exhilarating as manifesting can be, especially in the beginning, "The secret of *The Secret* is that it doesn't

make you happy," says spiritual teacher Adyashanti. Frustration and self-blame can arise because the present moment, even if it's good, doesn't match the visualization. And desires, even if met—especially if met!—have a way of gathering force to create more desires. Eckhart Tolle writes in *A New Earth*, "As long as [desire] runs your life, there are two ways of being unhappy. Not getting what you want is one. Getting what you want is the other." Paradoxically, moving in concert with the unfolding of events through divining does seem to deliver both peace of mind and outcomes that delight, partly because they arrive in unforeseen packaging.

That said, they need not be opposing approaches, and when combined in a particular way, they can work powerfully together, as Rick Jarow points out: "Divining is yin, receptive, and manifesting is yang, active—and they complement each other when they're used in sequence. First you divine to seek direction, and then you manifest that with clarity." By divining first, he says, you attune yourself to an underlying order, making ego aggrandizement less likely: "If you're not receptive to the forces, you're going to use manifesting as a pure power technology, which will create suffering for yourself and everyone else." He says that when divining is done with clarity and a pure heart, "it allows you to manifest clearly without creating ego chaos."

Once you use divining to know which direction to head, you can use it as a tool to help you manifest an outcome more efficiently. In chapters 7 and 8, for example, you'll find divining techniques that enable you to weigh options for action and to uncover unconscious blocks to success.

If you're attracted to manifesting, experiment to see what works for you. But do be clear about the differences between the two approaches and careful in how you mix them, lest a single-minded focus on reaching a goal contaminates the accuracy of your divining.

For You to Calculate: How Right Are Your Answers?

Are the answers always right? When I asked this question of some of the top kinesiologists and dowsers in the country, people with decades of steady practice, they typically told me that their accuracy rate was between 90% and 92%. "You are just getting the best answer that you can get in that moment," says Anne Williams, a top dowsing teacher in New York City. "It's not gospel. Nothing that you get is written in stone."

The wonderful thing is, 90% is a very high percentage. By comparison, stock-market investors who diligently follow analysts' reports make good choices only 50% of the time, and a 70% accuracy rate by a quantitative-analysis stock-market guru is seen as remarkable. Professional sports bettors are considered near-omniscient if they hit 70% on a regular basis.

And what is even more wonderful is that it's not 100%. It keeps us actively in the game. Otherwise, we could easily become automatons. "That 10% gives you a life," says kinesiology counselor Barbara Lubow. "If it weren't there, it's like your mother telling you what to do and you follow it—there's no growth in that, even if it is the highest mother of your own consciousness!" Instead, we have to constantly do double-checks at all levels—physical, mental, emotional, spiritual—to watch how things unfold and make sure that we're on track. The need to live out the answers to see if they're right keeps us in suspense, appreciative, and learning. And when the answers turn out to be wrong, usually that in itself is fruitful information: the ways in which our divining goes wrong are often the ways in which our life goes wrong.

Explains Darlene Van de Grift, "When you ask a question, it takes all the possibilities and probabilities that are known and unknown in the future about that situation and will tell you in that moment what the outcome of an action will be. You ask, *Should I do whatever?* It says Yes, and you start to head down that path. But as time goes on, you might find that something that needed to happen didn't, and what really mattered was the journey you took to get there. It's about the process itself: you've got to be fluid and free enough to not get locked into the outcome."

"The process is sacred, but the answers aren't," is the way my friend Kathleen Donovan puts it. Sometimes an answer is simply a stepping stone that gets you where you need to be so the next event can unfold and the next question can come up. Once when I was in India, I needed a haircut, and after muscle-testing and getting a firm Yes for a local beauty parlor, I headed there. Just outside the building, I ran into an Italian friend and—since my mind was tuned into haircuts—I noticed she had a really great one. She told me she had just gotten it from a British stylist who had worked at a top London salon and now occasionally cut hair in his flat, a few blocks away. I tested again—Yes! He gave me a really smashing cut, much friskier than I would ordinarily wear. The synchronicity of running into her gave me the push to hold the first answer lightly and flow with what was happening, rather than turning the first Yes into dogma.

Also, when we're evaluating the answer, we're doing it from our limited perspective, and sometimes the Universe has a broader picture. "It gets apparent over time that the answers you get are almost always either correct, or it's what the Universe wants," says Leroy Bull. He tells of a well-known dowser who tried to find water on the land of an older couple whose son was permanently stationed with the navy in Florida. The couple wanted to sell the land so they could move from Pennsylvania to be near him. Leroy double-checked his work and concurred that there was water there, but "when they drilled it, they got nothing—and that about busted their savings for a while," says Leroy. A year later, the couple was getting ready to try for a second well when they learned that their son had just been restationed—to Philadelphia, thirty miles away. "If they had gotten water, they might have been living in Florida by then," chuckles Leroy.

Divining also has an element of playfulness that can verge on trickiness. In Greek mythology, the god of the crossroads, Hermes, is also the trickster, and practically speaking, divining can occasionally give you answers that have you scratching your head and laughing. In one case, a famous dowser giving a lecture asked a pendulum to indicate what direction north was in, and it kept swinging east, toward the audience. It turned out that a Mr. North was sitting in the first row!

For You to Learn: How to Trust It

You might be one of those people who take to divining like a duck to water, with not a doubt about your ability to swim. But more often than not, people report being highly skeptical and being won over only because divining proved itself—sometimes with a dramatic incident, sometimes slowly over time, and often with both. The first time Marta Smith, who now teaches dowsing workshops, heard a dowser talking to her husband, she had to escape to the kitchen so they wouldn't see her laughing. Diane Bull, a biophysicist, was married to a prominent dowser, but it took her twenty years and a dire illness to start divining for herself. "I knew it worked for him, I just didn't believe it worked for me," she says. It can take a lot of proof to break through the deep conditioning of our minds and the left-brain bias of our culture, but if we keep with it, divining will supply that proof, over and over.

Most often, acquiring that trust takes time. It's the nature of the way trust is built in any relationship, bit by bit, day by day. Divining is different in one respect: trusting it is really trusting yourself. Over time, you may well come to see that it takes you to important places in life you wouldn't ordinarily go and that you learn things there that enrich your life and deepen your experience of your own divine potential. The more you experience that, the more trusting you become of the process and the more willing you are to receive its guidance. "It opens channels up because you're asking all the time, 'Please give me help,'" says Darlene Van de Grift. "You'll find the gems in every avenue you go down, and you'll start to learn that yes, it works out."

When you get a surprising answer, you'll often also get a gut-level "aha" feeling, a deep sense that it's the right way to go even though it runs counter to your opinion or brings up fear or resistance. Trusting and moving with it is like skydiving from a plane, but in that moment of trust we feel free and alive and truly ourselves. We break out of our straitjacket of conditioning, and the Universe catches us with open arms and gives us what we need next.

You can get good, solid answers from the very beginning just by taking a deep breath and plunging into it. And you will find that you get better at it over time, especially in queries in which you need to ask detailed, specific questions. Along the way, there may be a bump or two: this is a necessary part of the learning curve, and may ultimately be just as important in developing your craftsmanship as the smooth part of the ride.

There is one good way to see if divining is for you: try it out. The next part of this book gives you step-by-step instructions on exactly how to do that. See if it works. If it does, you have a helpmate for life. If it doesn't, no problem: you can sell this book on eBay!

PART TWO

HOW TO DIVINE

In the next six chapters, you will learn in-depth about muscle-testing and pendling; in chapter 10, you will learn about the chits.

The first two tools are bundled together because, once you get past the basic mechanics, they share many features and applications. What they have in common is that both relay information from the unconscious mind via neuromuscular movements. When you muscle-test, you can feel, often to your surprise, the muscles in your fingers strengthening when your nervous system sends a Yes and weakening when it sends a No. When you pendle, the tiniest of neuromuscular movements, transmitted from your unconscious, directs the pendulum's sway.

Both tools give you a straightforward Yes/No response, a binary pattern that serves as a divining digital code. This may seem limiting, but the wide universe of computer applications—from word and data processing to the web to satellite communication to artificial intelligence and beyond—is built on the same Yes/No code.

The range of possibilities with divining also seems infinite, and you'll start to experience that as you try out the instructions. You'll get immediate results, and you'll also find that as you build your skills—including focusing your mind and asking spot-on questions—divining can get richer and more complex, and can take you as deep and far as you want to go.

As you build your divining skills, you will progress through three stages:

- Learning. For muscle-testing and pendling, carefully follow the instructions in chapters 4 through 6 until the basics are second nature and feel totally natural to you. This may take a few days to a few months. As you learn to ask simple questions and get reliable answers, you'll develop confidence in yourself and the process. Then move on to the intermediate level, in chapter 7, where you'll learn how to systematically hone in on incoming information to make it more precise in order to compare options and plot courses of action.

- Mastering. Advance to chapter 8 to widen your skills by applying them to situations ranging from choosing a plumber to making a purchase. You can also deepen your divining with an interactive process called dialoguing, an on-the-spot Yoda that helps you sort through quandaries and change behaviors in yourself. In chapter 9, you can explore other kinesiology and dowsing tools.

In chapter 10, you'll learn about the chits, based on a random throw of folded pieces of paper. Although neuromuscular movements are also involved, this tool can better be understood in the context of classical forms of divining like the *I Ching* and the runes. Clarity and focus are still critical, but the chits don't require the same degree of skill building.

As you practice with these tools, if you run into roadblocks, the Divining Checklist in appendix 1 will help you pinpoint solutions.

- Transcending. The more comfortable and skillful you become, the more you'll find yourself putting your own fingerprints on the process so that it reflects your personality and needs. In that way, your innate creativity will allow you to transcend the forms, adding to the human volume of knowledge on what makes divining work.

WHICH TOOL SHOULD YOU USE?

As you read through the information, see which tool you are drawn toward, and experiment to see what works best. If you are choosing between muscle-testing and pendling, it is probably best to stick with one or the other until you develop the necessary skills and self-confidence; then you can easily expand your virtuosity to the other tool.

In practice, people seem to be guided intuitively or practically to use one over the other. Some top dowsers say they tried muscle-testing and it didn't work for them;

some muscle-testers had no luck with the pendulum. Other people have found that the two shade into each other. In fact, there are workshops at the American Society of Dowsers convention on body dowsing, which looks like muscle-testing, and deviceless dowsing, which resembles pure intuition. Some people use them and the chits selectively, depending on need; for example, they'll pendle for supplement choices, muscle-test for travel dates and car routes, and turn to the chits for guidance on a relationship.

I use different approaches to verify major decisions. When I recently returned from a brief trip to India, I was lying in bed in the morning and missing India's color and chaos. So I muscle-tested the question, *Will I go back for a long trip?* Yes. *How many months?* One, two, three . . . As the numbers kept going up, I was getting really nervous. Fifteen, sixteen, seventeen. *Starting when?* October, ten months away. This was too mind-blowing to take in, although deep down I was elated and it felt terrifyingly right. It took me several more months to absorb it, during which I double- and triple-checked it with muscle-testing. In January, in a sacred space, I lit a candle, threw the chits, and got: Go to India for seventeen months starting in October. As a final check—although I felt committed by then—I had a session with Darlene Van de Grift, my muscle-testing teacher, and she confirmed that it was what was needed next in my life. I packed up my house, put it up for rent, closed my business, and boarded the plane—and so I sit here now, with the sounds of raucous crows, tinkling bike horns, and flowing cadences of Tamil floating through the air. Very happy!

CHAPTER 4

MUSCLE-TESTING

LET YOUR FINGERS DO THE TALKING

I was going to a five-day silent retreat in California, and when I muscle-tested for dates, what came up was that I should spend another nine days in the Bay Area. I had several relatives and friends I wanted to see who were scattered around the area, but how to coordinate all of their busy schedules with mine? It would require many phone calls. So I tested. I got to see my Uncle Jack and Aunt Joyce in Fremont on Friday, Saturday, and Sunday; my cousin Katy and her boyfriend, Pablo, in San Francisco on Monday; my friend Martha in Walnut Creek on Tuesday and Wednesday; my friend Neal in Mill Valley on Thursday; my friend Suzie in Sonoma on Friday; and Katy and Pablo in San Francisco again on Saturday. It took about a minute. I made phone calls, and each person was available on their designated day, with one exception: Katy and Pablo would be out of town Saturday night. Puzzled, I made arrangements to stay in their San Francisco apartment by myself anyway. Everything worked out beautifully, and I was even able to write three health articles while hopscotching from place to place. As it turned out, I really needed that last night alone to decompress from all the visiting! I spent early Sunday morning sitting among the exotic orchids in the nearly empty Conservatory of Flowers in Golden Gate Park, a serene end to the trip.

When it comes to ease, versatility, and efficiency, the tool of muscle-testing can't be beat among divining options. These contribute to its quiet spread across the country, inspired by holistic medicine practitioners. It can do everything from picking out the best shampoo to pointing out deep-seated emotional blocks. It even comes with a fairly logical explanation of how it works, which helps the doubting mind accept its guidance.

As easy as it is to learn, it demands self-honesty, focus, and precision in its execution. It works best with both a serious intent and a light spirit.

Muscle-testing involves asking a question and getting a response by seeing whether a certain muscle holds its strength (Yes) or loses it (No). "Anybody can do it because it uses your electrical system and your muscles. If you are alive, you have these two things," says Machaelle Small Wright, who pioneered the muscle-testing method detailed in this book.

If you've ever gone to a chiropractor, dentist, or bodyworker who's asked you to hold up your arm while they try to pull it down, you've had the experience of muscle-testing, or kinesiology. Modern muscle-testing began in 1964 with George Goodheart, an appropriately named chiropractor who discovered that touching muscle reflex-points in certain ways provided information not just on muscular problems but on other health conditions as well, and that those muscles provided feedback on whether a corrective strategy had worked. His system, which he called Applied Kinesiology, was based partly on the energy meridians of Oriental medicine. It was further developed by chiropractor Alan Beardall, who expanded its use for diagnosis and treatment, and integrated it with other healing modalities, under the name Clinical Kinesiology. Another chiropractor, John Thie, developed a do-it-yourself muscle-testing system for the general public called Touch for Health, which could be used to assess a body's needs and correct imbalances. Kinesiology has since expanded in many directions—there are 150 types listed in one British database—and has grown increasingly sophisticated and specialized. Major branches include applied kinesiology, to treat physical and structural conditions; educational kinesiology, to help improve cognitive processing; health kinesiology, to counter stress and restore balance to the body; and creative kinesiology, for personal growth and expansion. Published studies have verified its physiological mechanisms, its usefulness in identifying allergies, imbalances, and illnesses, and the importance of skill building; health practitioners with five years' experience proved adept at getting reliable results.[1] (Note: applied or clinical kinesiology differs from the kinesiology taught in traditional health science courses, which involves the study of muscles and body movements.)

One of its variations is One Brain, developed by Gordon Stokes and Daniel Whiteside to treat dyslexia as well as emotional stresses underlying physical symptoms. The person who taught me muscle-testing, Darlene Van de Grift, was trained and worked professionally in that system as well as in Touch for Health. Another teacher of hers has been Machaelle Small Wright, a dynamo who founded Perelandra, a nature research center near Jeffersonton, Virginia. Wright developed and refined the finger-testing method of kinesiology, using it to communicate with nature intelligence and to test flower essences for healing. With simple, forthright language, she has demystified the matter. "Small children can learn to do kinesiology in about five minutes," she writes. Many of the how-to instructions in this chapter are based on her writings; the more elaborate variations in the following chapters have come via Darlene.

The Advantages of Muscle-Testing

The beauty of this tool is that you can use it quickly in almost any circumstance on any question. It is:

- Easy to learn. You can pick up the basic mechanics of it in less than an hour, maybe even less than ten minutes! Five minutes if you're a child.

- Versatile. In an orderly way, you can test many options and permutations to obtain information that is both thorough and specific.

- For even mundane questions. You can ask about such slight matters as what to wear and what route to drive to work, silly things that can over occupy our minds.

- Like a conversation. You can dialogue with it over time to think things through and come up with solutions.

- Easily personalized. Your beliefs, personality, and needs will shape your use of it so that it becomes your own unique system.

- Always evolving, as are you. As time goes on, you'll find that it changes as you change, as reflected in the depth and range of your queries.

The Drawbacks of Muscle-Testing

The biggest problem with this tool is that you can use it quickly in almost any circumstance on any question. Because it is almost too easy to use, your testing can become sloppy and your results will suffer. Also, it can be:

- Influenced by your emotions and desires. Any emotionally fraught or desire-laden matter is highly prone to "wishful testing." For example, asking a loaded question like, *Do I have cancer?* is bound to be an exercise in futility; even the thought of it can almost scare us to death, so it is tough to get into a neutral-enough state to receive whatever answer arrives. However, if you are careful to get quiet, connected, and especially neutral, you can minimize the influence of your emotions and desires. Blind-testing can also help you avert emotionally loaded distortions.

- Affected by fatigue and being off-center. If you're out of it, your results will be distorted.

- Irritating to others. Because it is visible, your friends and family may react in, shall we say, nonsupportive ways, especially if control is an issue for you or them.

Muscle-Testing Is Especially Good For . . .

- Purchases. Whether it's a computer or a watermelon, testing can quickly sort through options to give you the best choice. I ordered a Dell computer online this way. The testing pointed to a reliable workhorse model used by college students, and I followed the guidance reluctantly, tempted by glowing reviews to order a flashier, lighter model. My brother bought the second one, and when I saw it, I realized its screen was too small for the writing work I do.

- Menu choices. You can ask, for instance, which entrée is healthiest for your body, or which one will taste best. You may encounter new sensory adventures! Roberta Godbe of San Rafael, California, tests a rich dessert like chocolate cake to make sure it won't be unhealthy or keep her awake all night. "Sometimes it's okay for my body, and sometimes, if I've had a stressful day, my body doesn't have enough reserves to manage it," she says. Some people report putting their hands under the table to test food choices, and many report this as being one arena where they are apt to ignore the guidance and bear the consequences!

- Vitamins, minerals, and other supplements. You can line them up and test them on a daily or weekly basis to see if each one is what your body needs in the moment; you can also check for the dosages. In the same way, you can test essential oils and Bach Flower Remedies to address emotional blocks or expand your awareness.

- Scheduling. For trips, you can test to get dates, times, airplane flights, highway routes, hotels, and sights to see. For meetings, you can test for participants, timing, and places to meet. Some people divine to determine what highway exits to choose, and which hotels and restaurants to use. Once, muscle-testing for a place to eat Sunday breakfast on a long interstate drive, I took an exit in the middle of nowhere, turned right, and drove about ten miles on a deserted road parallel to the highway, wondering as the miles ticked off if I was truly nuts. The final Yes response brought me into the crowded parking lot of a lovely restaurant; inside were buffet tables overflowing with croissants, salmon, and raspberries. Whew!

- Selecting a professional. If you need a lawyer or doctor, you can open the phone book and work your way down the list. Be sure to be clear about what you want: for starters, someone who will work for your highest and best good. One friend simply asked for a doctor who wouldn't prescribe diagnostic tests. "He was very strange—like from another planet—but he never mentioned a test," she laughs. The next time she tested for a doctor, she added competence to her query!

- Sorting through the marketplace of ideas. With course catalog in hand, you can muscle-test for the class or workshop that is in your highest good to take. In a bookstore, you can use it to find the most useful book for you on a particular subject. And if you have a book full of tips and exercises on, say, finances or emotional healing, you can muscle-test to find which page has the information you most urgently need.

DARLENE VAN DE GRIFT
MUSCLE-TESTING IN ACTION

"Why do you have to be everybody's everything?" Darlene Van de Grift asked me, and all I could do was gape at her in shock. During a workshop, she had just used muscle-testing to help me identify an emotional block, and now she tested for the age when it had started—four. Yes, that was when my young, loving mother was at the limits of endurance. Besides me, she had a two-year-old, a one-year-old, and was again pregnant. I wanted with all my heart to help her with the babies, but couldn't do much, being four. Suddenly I understood why I literally ached to be of service to people, and that overwhelming, unconscious feeling lost its power and pain.

That's the kind of bull's-eye that I've seen Darlene, my muscle-testing teacher, hit again and again with clients. A master kinesiologist, she zeroes in on the exact origin of a problem with startling speed. And she has used muscle-testing itself to hone the clarity and self-honesty she brings to the process.

The first time she saw kinesiology in action—a chiropractor was treating her mother for terminal cancer—she was not impressed. "I was seventeen and it was, 'Yeah, yeah,'" she says. Her skepticism turned around when her mother, given six months to live by the hospital that had dismissed her, recovered fully and went into practice with the chiropractor as a massage therapist three years later. Darlene became a massage therapist herself and went on to teach it, as well as other emerging modalities, including Touch for Health and One Brain, both kinesiology-based. Along the way, she discovered that she could successfully muscle-test remotely for clients over the phone, using herself as a surrogate, something no one had taught her: "My whole body became attuned to muscle-testing because I was doing so much of it, and I realized that on an unconscious level, some part of my body was always testing."

But she didn't use it personally for another five years, and then only to seek spiritual guidance. Despite reading a lot of spiritual and channeled books, she felt dissatisfied: "It expanded me on a certain level, but I didn't want to get hooked on anything." Her testing led her quickly into her depths and revealed her major trauma. Her last five months in utero, her mother had been hospitalized for severe toxemia, and neither mother nor baby was expected to live: "I had to block out her feelings of fear and move forward or I was going to die. I was submerged and fighting for my life." Understanding that helped Darlene realize the depth of her love for her mother, which in turn made her a better mother to her three children. And she's seen how that early blocking out helps her block out the fear and other disabling emotions of her clients, enabling her to stay neutral and test more accurately.

Her use of muscle-testing has grown increasingly precise and sophisticated, and she often dialogues with it to explore all sides of a question or issue. "I've learned that it's not a blanket Yes or No for anything," she says. "I normally find a hundred questions to ask to make up my mind." For relationships, she says, "My biggest question used to be, *Will it last?* It would give me a time period and I would say, 'yeah, right,' and ignore it." Sure enough, it would end at that point, and soon she learned to ask other questions: *If it's got five years, is it of benefit for me to stay with him? How much? On what level? Okay, so if it's the spiritual level, is it karma? Lessons? For me? My children? Do I really need to have this relationship?*

On the day she turned forty, she woke up with the crystal-clear inner message that she had to close down her business in Pennsylvania and move her family to upstate New York. "I was like, 'No, I'm not,' and it was, 'Yes, you are.' I walked around for three days in shock." Muscle-testing advised that, among other benefits, each of her three children would meet someone in New York important to their futures and that she was to meet a man. Already in a relationship, she was aghast: "Oh no, I'm not doing this again!" Ten years later, she met Paul, the first man whose anger made her laugh instead of cringe, and they've been together ever since.

A dream gave her the idea for their health food store in an upstate ski town, which seemed the ideal way for Paul to leave his high-stress designer job in New York City. Muscle-testing was dour: it advised that stress levels would be 100%, success levels only 50% or 60%. "We were on a roll—he was quitting work—and it was, 'Don't give me any more information, I just know I need to do it,'" she says. Sure enough, after a year of false starts and a pricey renovation, their charming, light-filled store finally opened—but little snow fell, gas prices kept tourists away, and their vegan menu didn't find enough adherents. They closed the store down a year later, but their relationship grew stronger, she became more comfortable in a public position, and he had made the lifestyle transition he wanted. Now she is back to counseling full-time. He is cooking at a nearby Tibetan monastery, renewing his deep interest in that spiritual tradition.

Darlene, ever expanding, has added open-ended questions to her testing: *What do I need to do next? Is there something I need to be aware of now? Is there something blocking me?* "These questions provide direction and cut out side trips that distract me—they are streamlining my journey by at least 50%, and each day synchronistic events prove to me that it works," she says. "For that, I am grateful."

THE BASIC MECHANICS

Teach yourself this muscle-testing technique when you're by yourself and can relax and focus, without distractions. Much of the information is based on Machaelle Small Wright's work; you can find more detailed instructions at perelandra-ltd.com. These instructions are for right-handed people; reverse directions if you're left-handed.

1. Get into Position

Turn your left hand over so it's palm up. Lightly touch the tip of your thumb to the tip of your little finger (pinky) of that hand. This closes an electrical circuit. It may feel awkward at first. (If you have long nails, you can rest the thumb on top of the pinky.) These are called the "circuit fingers" (see figure 1). Then put the thumb and index (pointer) finger of your right hand together. These are the "test fingers" (see figure 2).

With the palm of your left hand facing you, put the "test fingers" inside that circle. It looks like a duck bill inside a hole. The outside knuckles of your right hand should be resting lightly on the inside knuckles of your left hand, whichever knuckles feel comfortable (see figure 3).

2. Calibrate for Yes

Ask yourself a Yes/No question for which the answer is undeniably Yes, such as:

Figure 1:
Circuit fingers

Figure 2:
Test fingers

Figure 3:
Testing position

Is my name _____ *[say your name here]?* (If there's any confusion in your mind about your name—for instance, if people call you by different names—ask *"Is my name my name?"* It sounds nonsensical, but it works!)

Is today _____*(the right day of the week)?*

Is my birthday _____*(your birthday)?*

For instance, you might be asking, *Is my name Jamie? Is today Tuesday? Is my birthday October 16? (assuming those are all true).*

Press your circuit fingers (the circle) lightly together, and using the same amount of pressure, push against them with the test fingers, trying to separate them. Use a steady, even pressure, not a pumping movement, and don't force it. You should find that the muscles will remain strong and the fingers won't separate. (Look at figure 3 on page 73 to see how the fingers stay closed.) Ask several more Yes questions, to get a strong sense of what that feels like in your fingers.

3. Calibrate for No

Then ask yourself a No question:

Is my name Mr. Potato Head?

Is my birthday February 30?

Am I ten feet two inches tall?

Press your test fingers against your circuit fingers, and this time the circuit should break and the fingers should open (see figure 4). Ask yourself some more No questions until you get a good sense of the way it feels. Be sure to keep the pressure equal in both fingers, and don't strain yourself by pressing or pushing hard. The gap may be small or wide, anywhere between a quarter-inch to several inches. Then go back and forth between Yes and No questions until you can easily discern the difference.

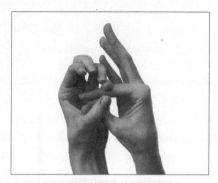

Figure 4: Calibrate for No

Those are the basics! If you're having trouble getting a response, switch hands and see if that works better. If you get the opposite response—your circuit fingers open on Yes and stay shut on No—don't worry, just go with that pattern. At some point, it may switch to the more standard pattern, or not.

There is one more pattern to train your fingers in.

4. Calibrate for a Choice

You'll use this when you want to select a choice from a list of options, such as online products or travel dates. Once you've established your Yes and No, ask your fingers: *Give me a Yes.* (Test.) *Give me a No.* (Test.) *Give me a Choice.* (Test, and see if your fingers open or close.)

To train yourself, ask the following questions out loud, holding the right answer in your mind:

Today is Monday, Tuesday, Wednesday, Thursday, Friday, Saturday, Sunday.

*This month is January, February, March, April, May, June,
July, August, September, October, November, December.*

As you go through the list, press your test fingers lightly against your circuit fingers for each item on the list. If you have determined that a choice is indicated by your fingers opening, they should stay closed as you individually test each option, and should open only when you come to the right answer. The opposite will be true if your fingers indicate that a choice is a closed circuit: as you check each option, your fingers will keep opening until you come to the right answer, and then they will stay closed. Either the open or closed response is fine—whatever your body tells you. Theoretically, closing on the answer makes more sense since it's a Yes, but practically speaking, if you're testing often, opening on the answer is less tiring.

Once you get the feel of it, you will be able to test almost anything in a minute or two. Although muscle-testing is useful immediately, it's best not to rush the process. Give yourself time to learn it thoroughly. Experts say that it typically takes about a year to learn the ins and outs of it, including how to ask questions in a way that gives you the answers you need.

If you can't get the Yes/No calibrations to work at all, it might be because you're overly anxious and tense, which blocks it. "Go ahead on to something else," Wright advises. "Then trick yourself. When you care the least about whether or not you learn kinesiology, start playing with it again. Approach it as if it were a game. Then you'll feel the strength and weakness in the fingers."

If you still find it's not working properly for you, you can try out other techniques to test with your fingers on pages 191–193; explore another tool like the pendulum or the chits; or consider using the supplementary approaches detailed in chapter 11.

One tip: see how lightly you can hold and push your fingers and still get a response. Otherwise, over time, you may strain those muscles, which will short-circuit your kinesiology development! If you find you're testing a lot, occasionally switch fingers or hands to avoid overtiring them.

EXERCISE
ASKING SIMPLE YES/NO QUESTIONS

For a few days, practice asking simple Yes/No questions to which you know the answers, until you feel comfortable with the simple hand mechanics of it. For example: *Is the time 10:30 a.m.? Do I have seven nephews? Are these socks black?*

As easy as muscle-testing is, there is another tool with a strong tradition behind it, and many practitioners accomplish remarkable divining with it. It is dowsing using a pendulum, or pendling. If you feel drawn to it, you'll learn in the following pages how you can use it along with, or perhaps instead of, muscle-testing—your choice. If pendling doesn't attract you, you still may find useful information to apply to your muscle-testing.

You can also skip the next chapter and go straight to chapter 6, "The Crux of It." There you will find the critical five steps that will assure you answers that ring strong and true for you on your path.

CHAPTER 5

PENDLING

SWING-DANCING WITH THE DIVINE

Cyndi Brush arrived at Home Depot only to discover that she should have measured the walk-in shower door opening in the home she was building. She told the sales assistant, "I drove an hour to get here and I'm not going back home to get the measurements!" Then she whipped out her pendulum. First she set up the parameters: she wanted a moderately priced door, functional, pleasing to look at, and one that she would be happy with. Then she dowsed for which catalog to look in—it turned out to be three inches thick—and then for the right page, which had lots of photos and measurement charts. "It had little tiny diagrams and one kind of lit up for me, so I dowsed it and got 10 on a 10-point scale," Cyndi recalls. The sales assistant warned her, "This will be a special order, so you won't get your money back." "That's fine," Cyndi replied. When it arrived, it fit perfectly and was just what Cyndi had wanted.

⌇

The pendulum is an ancient tool for divining, used throughout history in virtually all cultures. It's unexcelled for sorting through vast quantities of information to pinpoint precisely what we need. There's a big catch to it: we can easily influence it with our desires and opinions. But if we learn to neutralize those, the pendulum can be a wise counsel on matters large and small, from picking a sound system to finding lost items to figuring out the best way to ask for a raise.

WHAT IS PENDLING?

The pendulum is a tool used in dowsing. The word "dowsing" can bring to mind a farmer in overalls, forked stick in his hands, searching for water underground, but the definition from the British Society of Dowsers is much broader: "To search, with the aid of simple hand-held tools or instruments, for that which is otherwise hidden from view or knowledge."

An earth-based tradition, dowsing has historically been used with great precision to measure the depth and flow rates of water, oil, and gas. Tantalizing evidence of its use in ancient history is found in cave paintings and rock carvings in Algeria, Egypt, and Peru that date from 6000 BC to 2000 BC, and references to it are found in Greek, Arabian, and northern European folklore and legends. In the 1500s, Queen Elizabeth I imported German dowsers to locate tin mines in Cornwall. Reliable reports exist that British troops used dowsing during World War II to locate shot-down airmen, and that Australian, British, and Italian soldiers used it to find water sources in enemy territory. U.S. Marines located Vietcong tunnels and ammunition dumps with the aid of homemade dowsing rods. And oil companies such as Richfield Oil, Standard Oil, and Getty

Oil have routinely if quietly employed dowsers to help site drilling operations.

The most extensive study to date on dowsing was a massive ten-year study financed by the German government and published in the *Journal of Scientific Exploration,* a peer-reviewed journal published at Stanford University. It found that dowsers correctly identified water sources 96% of the time in directing the drilling of 691 holes in an area in Sri Lanka where the odds of finding water by random drilling were very low. The dowsers were able hundreds of times to predict the depth of the water source and the yield of the well to within 10–20%, which study author Hans-Dieter Betz, a physicist at the Ludwig Maximilian University of Munich, called "puzzling but enormously useful." He added, "We need to run a lot more tests, because we have established that dowsing works, but have no idea how or why."[1]

Compared to the array of handheld electronic devices we carry around today, dowsing tools are extremely simple. They can be coat hangers bent into L-shapes, or forked twigs. Among them, the pendulum—a hanging weight—is the most popular and portable. Historically, it has been used for such things as figuring out the cause of illness, finding a guilty culprit, and choosing the best course of action in love and business.

In effect, the pendulum amplifies messages from the unconscious that come via minute neuromuscular movements; it's like using a hearing aid to boost the volume of that still, small voice within. Just about everyone can get a pendulum to swing in response to questions, dowsing teachers report. Veteran dowser Leroy Bull says that of the three hundred people a day who walk into his dowsing booth at fairs and festivals, all but one or two of them can do it right off the bat, and those who can't are blocked only by tension.

The uses of dowsing are evolving over time, as can be seen in the popularity of topics at the annual conference of the American Society of Dowsers. Founded in 1960 in Danville, Vermont, the organization's original emphasis was dowsing for underground water veins and minerals, known as "information dowsing." The topic is still taught by practical, square-jawed engineers and farmers, although it occupies only 10–20% of the schedule. Getting really good at this type of dowsing requires two to three years of steady practice. With the right temperament, training, and dedication, you can meticulously develop the skills to do highly technical work.

In the 1980s, workshops in "household dowsing"— for practical, everyday concerns like purchases and food choices—entered the conference schedule. Tipi Halsey, for example, got hooked on dowsing when, seeking an eggplant-colored coat for a wedding, she pendled and learned, correctly, that it was at Macy's on the third floor, rather than somewhere at Bloomingdale's or JCPenney. If you're quiet, connected, and neutral, you can get good results with this kind of dowsing from the beginning.

These days, "energy dowsing"—healing diseases and adjusting energetic patterns in buildings and nature by using dowsing tools to communicate with other dimensions of existence—is the hot topic. This type of dowsing can be problematic and prone to imagination unless you're well grounded and trained by experts. It is not covered here, but you can find good books on the subject in the ASD bookstore.

Pendling can be so intriguing when you start learning it that one outcome is almost predictable: you'll pendle too much. It will drive your friends crazy, and maybe you, too. Don't worry: it's actually good training, especially in the beginning. Over time, you'll find yourself backing off, reserving pendling for those times when you truly don't have an answer. The nice thing about pendling, and divining in general, is that it's self-correcting. If you over-rely on it, it will push you away and start giving you answers that confuse rather than serve you.

The Advantages of Pendling

Once you get the hang of it (pun intended), pendling is:

- Easy to do. You can get a Yes/No reply within seconds.

- Efficient. It can be used to sort quickly through a large volume of options, especially if you use charts.

- Customizable. Whether you're meticulous or once-over-easy, you set it up in a way that works for your mind and personality.

- Easy to train in. A network of local and national dowsing organizations can give you expert guidance and support in building your skills.

The Drawbacks of Pendling

Alas, this powerful tool can be:

- Easily influenced by desires, aversions, emotions, and thoughts. Unless you get good at putting those to the side, you'll get poor results.

- Awkward to use in public places. You'll have to get used to incredulous stares if you use it out in the open, which is why some people develop strategies like using it below the table in restaurants. That isn't a problem for everyone. When Tom and Sandi Ruelke whipped out a pendulum in front of a truck salesman at a car dealership, "He was absolutely fascinated," says Sandi. Then again, they had pendled for the right salesman before they arrived!

Pendling Is Especially Good For . . .

- Finding a health practitioner. Before heading off to a hot springs, David pendled to select the gender and first initial of a massage therapist he might use there. "When I got there, they had photos posted, and the only guy whose name started with a *J* was an energy healer and no one I ever would have gone to—but it was one of the most miraculous experiences I had ever had in my life," David says. After two more equally profound sessions, he pendled and was advised to stop. "The intensity of the experience was such that I couldn't imagine not going to him for the rest of my life—but I was given to understand that he had limitations and had already given me what I needed," he says.

- Getting geographic information. Carolyn Touryniere of New York City pendled over a map to find a place to move where she would be safe, where she could heal emotionally from a setback, and where she could move closer to the best spiritual path for her. It turned out to be the Florida Keys, where she has been very happy.

- Food and vitamin choices. You can use it in the moment to assess what your body needs, as well as the amounts or dosages. Just for fun, go through your kitchen shelves with a pendulum, asking, *Is this healthy for my body?* I was surprised to find that the pricey Celtic gray sea salt from the health food store and the cheap iodized Morton Salt from Safeway both got a No, but the midpriced red seaweed-enriched salt from Trader Joe's got a Yes.

- Clearing a space of negative thoughts and energies. "Everything has energy, whether positive or negative," says dowsing teacher Anne Williams of New York City. "By clearing negative energy, we are neutralizing the energy so we can then transform it into something positive." To clear negative energy, she advises using a counterclockwise swing while saying, "I ask the Highest Universal Energy Source to neutralize any negative thoughts and energy that are adversely affecting the problem." When the pendulum comes to a halt, ask it to go clockwise and say, "I ask to transform these negative thoughts and energy to something beneficial." The pendulum stops as soon as this is done.

- Recovering lost objects. With the aid of maps and floor plans, it can be used to locate missing persons, pets, and things. To find a lost object, for example, you can pendle a floor plan of a house from a distance or walk from room to room pendling. Be sure to ask how far up from the ground an object is.

- Diagnosing mechanical problems. With the right chart (see *Pendulum Charts* by Dale W. Olson), you can zero in on your car's malfunctions. Then you take the car to a mechanic, pendling for the best one, if need be: "I dowse for which mechanic is best for me, my wallet, and my car," says Scot Foxx of Colchester, Vermont.

LEROY AND DIANE BULL
HOW DIVINING EVOLVES OVER TIME

When U.S. food inspector Leroy Bull walked into a slaughterhouse, wrongdoers had reason to worry. He had the knack of heading straight to the place where illegalities were underway: water being pumped into pork to increase its weight, unhealthy cows headed to slaughter. His information came before he set foot in the building. At his desk, he would take out a pendulum and dowse the floor plan of the plant to look for places where mischief was occurring.

Leroy, who recently retired after forty-one years, is one of the foremost dowsers in the United States and a former president of the American Society of Dowsers. Solid, straight talking, and laid-back, he began dowsing at age twelve the old-fashioned way: forked stick in hand, searching for underground water veins. In college at Penn State, studying animal husbandry, he met and married a science student with a husky laugh named Diane. She prized rationality and was to become a research biophysicist. "The only way the Universe could have gotten us together was on a blind date," she says. "I certainly wanted nothing to do with him until he kissed me." She would go with him to dowsing conventions and could even pinch-hit teaching pendling if there was an overflow of students, but she never really believed in it for herself—until she got hit with chronic fatigue so severe she felt herself hovering near death. Too exhausted to overrule it with her mind, she pendled for essential oils every morning, and then saw at day's end how a particular oil protected her from an unwise food choice or a negative encounter with someone. Slowly but surely, aided by a life-changing trip to an ashram in India, she recovered.

Their daughter, Sarah, used to ask her father to dowse when she lost a sneaker. But when she turned eleven or twelve, he stopped getting answers; it was her turn to locate them with dowsing, which came naturally to her. "It's really cool to see how smart the Universe is," Leroy chuckles. Now a physicist in the field of medical imaging and radiotherapy, she fills in for Leroy when he has too much water-dowsing to do, and is careful to carry a dowsing tool with her. "She can easily do without one, but if people see a pretty young woman drive up in a red sports car, jump out, and point straight at the spot, they won't believe it," he says.

About twenty-five years ago, after twenty-seven years of dowsing, Leroy no longer needed a tool; having dowsed for hundreds of wells, his accuracy rate is a remarkable 95%. Ten years ago, he started seeing underground water veins as golden lines running in the grass. "And where one or two of them cross, there's going to be a little computer animation where they're going blink blink blink—and that's where the well goes," he says. The clear, neutral space in which answers come is second nature to him now, and when he asks a question, he sees a yellow smiley face for a Yes, a yellow frowning face for a No. He trusts the answers, especially those that aren't logical: "Then you know your rational mind didn't get in the way."

For her part, Diane will dowse for food choices, but in the rest of her life, she says, "I go where my feet take me." She doesn't try to figure things out in advance, even with pendling. "At first the process bothered me a lot because I wondered, am I really weird? And I would argue with it. Then I just got used to it and found that if I could allow myself to follow my feet, it would bring me great joy," she says. At the egg section in the supermarket, where she finds herself headed in spite of not needing eggs, she meets someone who needs a comforting presence; taking an out-of-the-way side road, she learns later she missed an accident; buying a stone pendant she doesn't like, she later meets someone who needs that exact thing.

In both of them, you can sense a deep serenity and joy and presence. They are fully alive and engaged. Divining, says Leroy, quiets the mind because "you're tuned into what's real rather than the shoulds, must-haves, and gottas that society is teaching you."

LEARNING THE BASIC MECHANICS

Because pendling has been in wide use for a longer time than muscle-testing, it has a much larger body of information available, with many books, courses, and websites. Some pendling instructions are very precise and technical, with detailed programming routines. An excellent example of this is the classic *Letter to Robin: A Mini-Course in Pendulum Dowsing,* by famous dowser Walt Woods. Other approaches are simpler and free-flowing, such as those explained in *The Divining Mind* by T. Edward Ross and Richard D. Wright. Like muscle-testing, pendling is ultimately an individual's play of consciousness, which is why advice often conflicts, even among two speakers in the same workshop at a dowsing convention.

What follows, then, is a simplified form of commonly given instructions for pendling. Remember as you read it that "No technique is set in stone: there are many approaches for many people," says Tom Graves, author of the very helpful *The Diviner's Handbook* and *The Dowser's*

Workbook. If you want to refine your techniques, the books listed in appendix 2 are a good place to start. The instructions in this book will help you dive right into the experience, and in the three chapters that follow, you'll learn how to put the mechanics to use in asking questions, how to hone in on information to make it more specific, and how to use advanced techniques like dialoguing, charts, and maps.

Although you don't have to believe in pendling for it to work, it helps greatly if you can suspend disbelief and approach it with an open, curious mind. Tanya Tkach of Quebec, Canada, tried pendling off and on for twenty years and was thoroughly convinced it wouldn't work for her, until a friend told her that it was her very disbelief that was blocking her ability. She tried again. "It started swinging so wide that I had to hold it way out from me because it had a long chain," she says. "I kept saying, 'Oh my God, oh my God.' When you do finally open up, it works. I think that's all dowsing is—opening up and letting the information come in."

FIRST STEPS TO PENDLING

1. Get Thyself a Pendulum

You can easily buy a pendulum at a health food store, gift shop, or jeweler. Simple ones can cost as little as two dollars, and elaborate ones a hundred dollars or more. No need to overspend: there is no correlation between price and effectiveness, and materials don't really matter, either. At some pendling classes, students use a screw nut on a string, and some pendlers stick with this five-cent solution. Ideally, the chain should be about five or six inches long, and the pendulum should end in a point, especially if you use charts or maps (see figure 5).

If you'd rather try this tool out before you invest, look around your house. You can get accurate results with any weighted object hanging from a string or chain, such as a pendant on a necklace chain, a large finger ring on dental floss, or a heavy key hanging from a string.

2. Calibrate It

Because a pendulum can swing many directions (and if your pendling starts getting wacky, you'll see just how many!), it's

Figure 5: Pendulum

important to pin down which swing means Yes and which swing means No. You can do this in two ways: by asking it or directing it. Either one works. In effect, in this play of consciousness, you're setting up the rules for communication between your conscious and unconscious mind.

If you have a laid-back, go-with-the-flow style, try asking; if you are a take-charge type, try directing. In practice, interestingly, women seem to prefer asking, men directing, but your style may differ.

In both these cases, make sure you're alone in a place that's quiet and where you won't be interrupted for a while. Close your eyes if it helps you to concentrate. Some experts counsel sitting at a table or in an armchair on which you can rest your elbow; some say it's better not to cross your hands or legs or let them touch each other.

Asking

With this approach, you are letting your unconscious program the pendulum in the way it sees best; you are the alert, interested observer.

Holding the string or chain about three or four inches up from the pendulum, ask it to show you how it swings to say:

Yes

With a focused mind, ask out loud or silently, *Please show me a Yes.*

Watch the direction the pendulum moves: it could be clockwise, counterclockwise, left to right, forward and backward, or sideways at an angle. Do not move your fingers; instead, simply observe it. If it takes a minute or two, stay with it, breathing deeply to relax.

No
Ask, *Please show me a No.* Observe the direction.

Neutral
Ask, *Please show me a Neutral.* This will be where your pendulum hangs out in your hand between questions. It may be motionless or swing at a particular angle. Later, when you ask a question and it doesn't move much from this position or swing, it could mean that the question is worded wrong, that you are taking the wrong tack, that the timing is wrong, or that the information is not available.

Now run it through its paces by asking it several Yes/No/Neutral questions like the following ones, until the swing is strong and true for each. Between each question, watch it return to Neutral, or touch it lightly to your other hand or another surface to stop it. Then try some questions of your own that you already know the answers to.

Yes:
Am I currently located in_____ [your state or country]?
Am I _____[your age] years old?
Am I in my_____ [home, office, wherever you are]?

No:

Am I currently in Antarctica?

Am I 209 years old?

Am I rollerblading at this moment? (Unless you are.)

Neutral:

Is it raining or snowing in Finland and Brazil today?
    (Poorly worded question.)

Where is that sock that I lost three years ago?
    (Can't be answered by Yes/No.)

If your pendulum is now in good working order, skip the next section and proceed to "Getting in the Swing of It" on page 96.

Directing

With this alternative, you are training your pendulum to move in certain directions using the power of your mind; essentially, you're training your unconscious mind to speak clearly to your conscious mind. It can be startling to see that by simply willing it, you can make a physical object move—and it's also useful in understanding how a strong mental preference can unwittingly color your pendulum response.

First, decide how you want your pendulum to swing. Two options are:

Directing #1 (Figure 6)
Yes: clockwise circles (like the second hand on a watch)
No: counterclockwise circles (the second hand going backward)
Neutral: a 45-degree swing

Figure 6: Directing #1

Directing #2 (Figure 7)
Yes: forward and backward (like nodding the head)
No: left to right (like shaking the head)
Neutral: a full stop in the middle

Holding one of the options in mind, hold the pendulum by the string and say, "This means a Yes." Wait and watch it. If you don't get a response in ten or fifteen seconds, nudge it by gently moving your fingers, but then stop and let it move on its own. You can hold it over the diagrams if that is helpful in training it.

Figure 7: Directing #2

Now say, "This means a No." Again, it should move on its own, but nudge it if necessary. Say, "This means a Neutral." Watch it swing at an angle (#1) or stand still (#2).

Using the questions on pages 93-94, run it through a series of Yes/No/Neutral questions, and then add a few of your own, until the swings are strong and clear without any conscious movements on your part. If it's not happening quickly, don't worry; just keep at it. Sometimes it takes time to forge these neuromuscular links.

That's it! Simple!

GETTING IN THE SWING OF IT

Until pendling becomes second nature to you, it is helpful to put a pendulum through its calibration swings each time you bring it out to ask some questions.

With practice, you'll see that one measure of the strength of a Yes or No is how energetically the pendulum swings. Sometimes you'll get a Yes so anemic the pendulum barely moves; other times it will almost jump out of your hand with enthusiasm. One way to observe this is to test the foods in your kitchen one by one, holding your pendulum over each and asking, *Is this food healthy for my body?*—remaining neutral as best you can if it gyrates madly over the cauliflower but dawdles at the croissants.

Some dowsers, especially those who work professionally, "program" their pendulums almost as one would a computer by reading to it a list of detailed instructions, such as that "time" refers to "my perceived time unless otherwise requested." This process pinpoints definitions between the conscious and unconscious mind and minimizes the chance of misunderstandings. It can become very complex indeed: one well-regarded engineer speaking at a recent ASD convention had a half-inch-thick notebook of programs that he renewed once a year with his pendulum. This approach is not for everyone, and by and large, it is best for us to keep things simple so as to minimize confusion and mental nattering. But if your mind tends toward the technical or detailed and you wish to undertake precision work, you may find these techniques valuable.

If you're having trouble getting the pendulum to work, it could be a case of performance anxiety. Especially in the beginning, our anxiety about getting it right can impede the natural flow of pendling. "Ask it to work. Don't tell it to work," advises Bruce Irwin. Relax, have a cup of coffee or tea, then try again. Or try a strategy advised by Tom Graves: work hard at it for several weeks, then give it up and come back to it later. The break will allow the information to coalesce in your brain without your conscious effort. "It's like 'proofing' the dough for a loaf by kneading it hard, then allowing it time to rise before kneading it again," he says.

Don't be afraid to be playful and experiment; that can loosen up anxiety. For example, you'll find that almost any hanging weight can be a pendulum, even a computer mouse hanging from its cord. The mother-in-law of a friend of mine, a ninety-one-year-old great-grandmother in Brooklyn, swings her shoulder bag at a street market to check which vegetables are ready for eating. Arthur Bailey, former head of the British Society of Dowsers, reports in *Anyone Can Dowse for Better Health* that he once saw a woman in a tea shop take a toy mouse out of her purse and dangle it by its tail over the scones to make sure they were made with butter rather than margarine!

EXERCISE
ASKING SIMPLE YES/NO QUESTIONS

Spend two to three days asking the pendulum simple questions that you already know the answer to until you're confident of a clear and rapid Yes/No response. For example: *Is this shirt white? Is it June? Is this meal my breakfast? Is today Tuesday?*

CHAPTER 6

THE CRUX OF IT

POPPING THE QUESTION

Now that you know the simple mechanics of muscle-testing and pendling, you have the key to turn the ignition in the vehicle called divining. You could start driving immediately, but it's worth your while to spend time learning skills systematically so you can avoid the fate of a four-year-old boy in Sand Lake, Michigan. He got behind the wheel of his mother's car late at night, started it, and drove it a few blocks to a video store, although he could barely see above the dashboard or reach the accelerator. When he saw the store was closed, he drove back home, hitting two parked cars before he was intercepted by a policeman whose attention was drawn by the weaving of the apparently driverless vehicle.

Divining is like that. It's so simple that you can, right at the start, get it to work. But you'll get further if you know more: where you want to go, where to make the turns, how to respond to unexpected events, what to do if you get lost. When you first learn to drive, you're excruciatingly conscious of every small detail (unless you're this child!). But when you get really good at it, you can fly through heavy traffic, feeling in the flow and free.

Just as a driving manual with all the rules and procedures of the road may seem daunting before you pass the driving test, so these instructions may seem complicated at first glance. But you'll find as you go through them that the process is very simple at its heart, and very quickly you will be divining with ease and getting the answers you need within minutes.

THE FIVE ESSENTIAL STEPS

Across cultures and continents, divining has evolved to include elaborate forms, rituals, and procedures that have given anthropologists many fruitful hours of study. For the simple, everyday tools of muscle-testing and pendling, the process here is pared down to five basic steps:

1. Get quiet.

2. Get connected.

3. Get neutral.

4. Pose the question.

5. Receive the answer.

For a really important decision, it may take you thirty minutes to cover all the steps. For a "What vitamin should I buy?" kind of choice, it might take a few seconds.

As rapid as this process can be, it pays to go slowly and deliberately through the first three steps—getting quiet, connected, and neutral—until they are embedded in your divining behavior and become second nature. This will ensure accurate, useful results, and once you get some practice, you'll be able to drop into that relaxed, receptive state in seconds.

This five-step sequence may change over time depending on your tool, your thinking style, and how important your question is. For instance, if you need to get practice at asking pointed questions, writing your question down on paper might be the first step. Getting quiet, connected, and neutral might require three distinct internal movements, or you might do them simultaneously, especially as you get more skillful. You may find that it works to neutralize yourself after posing the question, rather than before.

In the two chapters that follow this one, you'll find midlevel and advanced instructions on how to apply these steps to get more detailed and wider-ranging information. After that, you'll find information on the chits, a simpler approach useful in weighty matters.

WALK-THROUGH: WHAT POPPING THE QUESTION MIGHT LOOK LIKE

Let's say you're undecided about what to do on your next vacation—so much world, so little time! Below is a scenario to demonstrate how you might sort through options using the basic procedures that you'll be learning in this chapter.

Getting Quiet

Take three deep breaths while sinking into your solar plexus. (This is just one example of a quieting technique; you might find better ones for yourself in the following pages.)

Getting Connected
Focus on your heart, feel it soften and open, and say, *I invoke the Light within, and I dedicate this to the highest good of all* (for example).

Getting Neutral
Mentally put everything to the side while saying silently, *Please remove all previous thoughts* (for example).

Posing the Question / Receiving the Answer

Tool Check

Give me a Yes.

Give me a No.

Asking Permission

Can I ask this question now? (Am I physically, emotionally, mentally, and spiritually able to get an accurate answer?)

May I ask this question now? (Is the timing right?)

Should I ask this question now? (Is it in my best interest to know the answer?)

The Crux

Is it in my highest good to take my two-week vacation this year? Yes.

Should I take it all at one time? Yes.

Should I take it in June? No.

July? No.

August? Yes.

Should I start it the first week? No.

Second week? Yes.

Should I go to Yosemite? No.

The Maine coast? No.

The Wisconsin Dells? No.

Montana? Yes.

Should I go to a dude ranch? No.

Go river rafting? Yes.

Will I find the best company for that by searching the Internet? No.

Asking my friend Michael how to get in touch with his friends in Missoula? No.

Reading outdoor magazines? Yes.

Which magazine will be most useful in giving me the information I need for this trip—Outside? No.

Backpacker? No.

Field & Stream? No.

Mountain Gazette? Yes.

Montana?! As you sit with the new information, say a simple prayer of thanks.

We'll carry this imaginary conversation forward in the next two chapters.

STEP 1: GET QUIET

Divining works most powerfully when we move out of our chatty, workaday, busybody mind and enter into a different, deeper space. Getting quiet, inside and out, is how to start that process. In effect, we're deliberately slowing down our brain waves so that we can access wider, deeper swaths of consciousness. Systems theorist Ervin Laszlo suggests that when we enter these more relaxed states, we increase the "bandwidth" of quantum waves to which our brain is receptive.

Find a place in which you can breathe deeply, free of interruptions and distractions. Sitting on a meditation cushion or church pew works, and so does sitting in a favorite chair in a quiet spot of the house, or with a cup of tea at the kitchen table, or even in your car, hopefully parked on a quiet side street. At work or around town, a bathroom stall can do just fine in a pinch.

The more important the question, the greater the need for silence and perhaps a small ritual, like a prayer and the lighting of a candle. For those times, choose the quietest time of day for you, such as early morning or late evening. For less than earthshaking questions, quiet surroundings are helpful when you are first learning; with time and practice, you'll be able to divine in a hubbub.

A straightforward way to quickly quiet yourself is to:

1. Close your eyes, which cuts out 78% of sensory stimuli.

2. Take three slow breaths so deep that the bottom of your diaphragm moves.

3. With each breath, sink deeper and deeper into your core self, behind your navel.

Some other simple techniques you might want to try are:

- Visualizing a scene or object that makes you feel peaceful and centered, such as ocean waves lapping a beach, a moonlit lake, or a field of wildflowers shimmering in the breeze.

- With your mouth softly closed, press your tongue lightly against the roof of your mouth and slowly let your jaw drop of its own weight, without any effort on your part, until your jaw hangs slack.

- Fix your attention on a cloud and breathe deeply as you watch it float along for a minute or two.

If time is not of the essence, you can also slow yourself down and put yourself into a silent space by, for example:

- Putting on melodic music with a languid rhythm, such as Schubert's "Ave Maria" or Estonian composer Arvo Pärt's "Für Alina."

- Starting with your toes and moving on up through your body, tightening and then relaxing each set of muscles.

- Rocking in an easy chair.

- Doing a few languid yoga stretches. One that is especially good for clearing the head is to sit cross-legged on the floor, clasp your hands behind your back, and lower your head forward, as though trying to touch the floor. In that position, observe the weight of your head slowly stretching your spine. When you straighten up, the mind is clearer.

- Petting a dog or cat.

- Sipping a hot drink while gazing at flowers, a garden, or trees.

An effective way to both calm and center yourself is four-corner breathing, suggested by psychologist Lucy Jo Palladino in *Find Your Focus Zone*:

1. Using a square or rectangular object like a door or window, look at the upper left-hand corner and inhale to a count to four.

2. Move your gaze (without moving your head) across to the upper right-hand corner and hold your breath to a count of four.

3. Move your gaze straight down to the lower right-hand corner and exhale to a count of four.

4. Then move your gaze to the lower left-hand corner, silently saying the words, "Relax, relax, relax," and do just that. Return your gaze to the upper left-hand corner. Repeat once or twice.

STEP 2: GET CONNECTED

Now that you're quiet, get in touch with that aspect of the Divine that resonates most deeply with you: your higher self, God, the Light Within, Presence, Love, cosmic consciousness, angels, a spiritual teacher or saint, guides, your wise self, your intuitive self. What is important is the feeling of inner connection, which ideally is kinesthetic and emotional as well as mental. You might feel an inner click or deep stillness or stirring of the heart or opening of the chest, or it might be a feeling of an inner shift, a subtle deepening, or a wave of relaxation. It can take just a second, or if you're wound up about something, it may require more time and effort. At one point, when I was muscle-testing frequently, I rushed past this point, and found that my results deteriorated. You don't want to wave carelessly to your Source as you pass by; you want to make a meaningful contact, however brief.

A common way to make that connection is by saying words silently or out loud that are meaningful to you—a prayer, an invocation, a chant, soothing phrases—while focusing mentally on an image of the concept or being. For example, you could pray the Lord's Prayer, the Twenty-Third Psalm, the Hail Mary; you could repeat a phrase or mantra like "Lord have mercy," "Shalom," "Peace," "Shanti," "Love," "Om Namah Shivaya," "Om Mani Padme Hum," "Kyrie Eleison," "Insha'Allah," "God willing," "God be with me"; or you could intone several slow Oms.

You can also say a special divining prayer that you compose yourself. For example, before she pendles, Anne Williams of New York City says:

"I invoke the light within. I am a clear and perfect channel. Love and light are my guides. They are with me and work through me at all times."

Ed Stillman, a dowser in Sedona, Arizona, always starts with:

"Lord, guide my hands and prepare my mind. Help me form my question with clarity. Enhance my sensitivity and bless my purpose for only the highest good that I may be an instrument of your power and glory in locating what I'm searching for. Amen."

If you have no particular personification of the Divine, you can reach that deepest and truest part of yourself by closing your eyes and using one of these approaches:

- Focusing on your heart while thinking of someone or something you love unconditionally. Even a pet works.

- Feeling the pervasive space that flows through you and everything else.

- Imagining a candle in the center of your heart and see it emanating a light that grows stronger and larger by the moment, until it fills your chest, then your body, then the room, then the world, then the Universe.

Carolyn North, author of *Synchronicity: The Anatomy of Coincidence,* uses this approach: "I inhale and feel everything from every direction and every dimension coming into me through my skin, the way you feel sunlight as it tingles and warms you. Then I exhale and transmit love outward, making an intention with my heart that what I am doing be for the good of all."

Dedicating It to the Highest Good
A simple and direct way of "cementing" that connection is to dedicate your divining session to the highest good, either silently or out loud.

Divining works most powerfully—and in the long run, only—when you do it for the highest good of yourself and others. "If you're working for the highest good, you're always working in a divine light. You're always connecting to Source," says longtime dowser Cyndi Brush. Without this firm intention, your ego can slip in and run the show, and if that happens, "You'll just create the exact image of all your impulses and compulsions and desires. You'll just re-create your basic mess," says Rick Jarow. You can reinforce this intention in two ways:

- When you divine, before asking the question, say an invocation, such as:

  I dedicate this to the highest good.

  May this work for the highest good of all.

  May this be for the highest good of myself, the other person, and all life in the Universe.

  I invite the answers that will work for my highest good.

- Or when you're asking a question, you can use the words in the question itself:

Is it in my highest good to buy this particular model of digital camera?

Is it in the best and highest good of all that we move into a smaller house?

STEP 3: GET NEUTRAL

This is the tricky part. And it's critical. In divining, we move our "little self" out of the way so that our "wise self" can come through. That "little self" or ego is full of opinions, judgments, and emotions, and it wants its way, no matter what. It's tricky and can interfere with the accuracy of divining in obvious and subtle ways.

That is why it's important to actively neutralize our ego and opinions. It is especially important when we have a preference about the outcome, which, since we're human, is more likely than not.

"Divining works through your subconscious mind, and one of the jobs of the subconscious is to please you, so let your subconscious know that the only way you are pleased is if it tells you the truth," says Marty Cain, who runs the beginning dowsing school at the annual American Society of Dowsers convention. "Because even good friends aren't always totally honest, and also because I may want a certain answer, I ask my pendulum to 'Tell me the truth,' so it becomes one place I can trust that I won't be lied to."

Being willing to hear the truth, no matter what it is, means stepping aside from the part of ourselves that wants things a certain way. Even if that moment of detachment is ever so brief, it can be freeing in other parts of life, too.

Psychology researchers have found that strong emotions and prejudgments hamper our ability to made sound decisions on a conscious level, and also warp input from the unconscious. When we learn how to put that little self aside, on the other hand, the Divine can more easily emerge. Studies of successful healers show that after an intense initial focus, they consciously move into a "type of surrender, a letting go of the self as well as of the outcome," writes Lynne McTaggart in *The Intention Experiment*.

Following are some mental, physical, and emotional ways to move yourself into a neutral, unattached place, a state of "high indifference," as Leroy Bull calls it. You can use them separately or combine some of them—whatever works best for you:

- Sink deep into a silent meditative place. "It's the feeling of going deep inside myself where there is no thought and no judgment. I'm breathing from that space, and I'm listening," says Gailann Greene, a holistic health consultant in Montclair, New Jersey.

- Say intently, *Please remove all prior thoughts* to clear the mental space.

- Put everything in your mind to the side, the same way you would if you had to quickly respond to an emergency. Just as your to-do list and last night's argument become meaningless if something urgent arises, clear your mind of extraneous clutter so you can focus 100% of yourself on the question at hand.

- Pray, "Thy will be done." Really feel it so that surrender to whatever the answer will be permeates your body. This prayer is so powerful that it is two to four times more effective than prayers that ask for a specific outcome, studies have demonstrated.

- Make your priorities crystal clear to your subconscious. Mentally put your desires to the side and say, front and center, *Please tell me the truth, and only the truth, on this.*

- Settle into an empty space that is simultaneously inside and outside yourself. "It's as though one eye is focused inside and one is looking wide," says Barbara Lubow.

- Ask yourself, "Do I really know it all? Do I really know what's good for me?" Think back over times you were convinced of a certain path or choice, and it turned out badly. Recall times when you were convinced something would not work out, and it did. You can even go a step further and ask yourself, "What do I know about anything, really?" "In my mind, I know that I am such a little consciousness that I don't know the answers. I really don't," says Gailann Greene.

- Ask yourself, "I really need this outcome—is it true?" Go deep and see where this question takes you.

- If you're weighing two options, put your hands palm up in front of you, about a foot apart, and mentally put one option in the left hand and the other in the right. Slowly move them toward each other, allowing them to talk back and forth if that comes naturally. Fold your hands together as they touch each other, and move your clasped hands to the middle of your chest, your heart.

- If you're hoping for a certain answer, think of ways in which the other option would work out just as well. If, for example, you're sorely tempted to buy a pricey new gadget-rich washing machine or lawn mower to replace an older one that is lumbering along just fine, play down the tempting purchase by imagining how broke and maybe guilty you'll feel afterward, and play up the old standby by recalling how it's always served you well.

- Play with options visually in your mind until the two equal each other in intensity, size, and proximity. For example, the old washing machine or lawn mower may seem smaller or dimmer or grayer or farther away; adjust those qualities until it matches the other one.

- On the floor in front of you, visualize a circle full of empty space; step into it and feel its qualities pervade you.

- Ask the question in the third person. Says Ed Stillman, "I dowse for a client named Ed Stillman, as though I'm standing apart from him—physically, mentally, and emotionally removed from everything associated with him." So if your name is Casey Smith, instead of asking, *Is this the machine that best answers my needs?* you would ask, *Is this the machine that best answers Casey Smith's needs?*

- Imagine you're sitting in an IMAX movie theater and everything you see and hear is a movie you can't take your eyes off of. Although you're deeply engaged in viewing what is happening, you're simply an observer. (This is also a novel way to walk down the street.)

- Be direct with the Divine. Say frankly, "I really need to know the answer to this question. Please do not allow my own thoughts and desires to get in the way of accuracy."

Once you have found what works for you to shift into that impartial state, you can move into it more quickly by "anchoring" it in your body with a certain physical gesture: clicking your heels together like Dorothy in *The Wizard of Oz*, snapping your fingers, running a finger over your cheek, rubbing your hands together, pulling your earlobes, running your hands over your head. To train your mind in this way, close your eyes and make the gesture at a time when you are firmly in that neutral state, repeating it several times. Release the anchor by opening your eyes and distracting yourself in some way. Repeat two or three times, each time making the feeling of "high indifference" more vivid.

If you can't get into a neutral space, be honest with yourself about it; it will save you from a skewed answer.

Consider putting off the question until you feel calmer, perhaps after taking a walk or shower, or several days down the road. You can also blind-test with a friend or on your own (see page 132), or use the chits, which can't be easily influenced by feelings and preferences.

GETTING HEAD, HEART, AND BODY INTO THE ACT

Divining is extremely potent when you engage all three aspects of yourself in the process: head, heart, and body. Before you actually ask the question, do a quick check: is your mind engaged, your heart open, your body feeling sensations? If all three are on deck, you're less likely to be out of balance—nervously mental, overemotional, or ungrounded, any of which can sabotage your results.

There's a wonderful process developed by psychologist Judith Blackstone, PhD, author of *The Enlightenment Process*, that engages all three aspects simultaneously. It puts you into a deep space for divining or meditating—or living life. It goes like this:

1. With your eyes closed, slowly move the focus of your attention from your toes to the top of your head, feeling that you are in each part of the body as you move through it. Then feel that you are inside your entire body all at once.

2. Mentally find the space outside your body.

3. Experience that the space inside and outside your body is the same continuous space. It pervades you.

4. Now attune yourself to the quality of awareness, or clarity, in your body by bringing your focus to your shoulders, head, and the space above your head. Experience that quality of awareness pervading your entire body and the whole environment.

5. Now attune yourself to the quality of emotion. This will be a different experience than the quality of awareness. It might be described as a change in texture, or weight. You will be attuning to this quality through the middle part of your body, the torso. Experience that quality of emotion pervading your body and the whole environment.

6. Now attune to the quality of physical sensation, bringing your focus down to the bottom third of your body, the pelvis and legs. Experience that quality of physical sensation pervading your entire body and the whole environment.

7. Attune to the qualities of awareness and physical sensation at the same time, pervading your whole body and environment. Now add in the quality of emotion, so that all three qualities are pervading your whole body and environment.

8. Sit quietly in this rich field for a moment, allowing your breath to glide through the space without disturbing your attunement to it.

STEP 4: POSE THE QUESTION

This is the heart of the matter, and where it's possible to go off base. In divining, as in life, the answers we get are as good as the questions we ask, so it's key to find the words that hit the mark. Some people are skilled at asking questions clearly and succinctly, but for many of us it takes practice. The learning process is useful in itself: sharpening a question sharpens our thinking, and sometimes that alone is enough to give us the insight we need.

First we'll look at the basics of how to word a question, and then we'll look at how to ask it during the divining process.

Composing the Wording

Your question must be short, sharp, and focused. It must be answerable with a simple Yes or No. If it's too long, complicated, or fuzzy, you'll get useless answers.

Try limiting yourself to a few words. Beware of the words "and" and "or," which indicate complex thoughts.

If you have trouble asking pointed questions, write your question down, especially at first, and record the answer. Also try asking the question out loud, which can help you articulate it better.

Some examples:

NO: *Is this a good vitamin C?* (Way too vague. Do you mean good value, good price, good ingredients, good manufacturer?)

NO: *Is this vitamin C the best choice for me, or is it better to get a cheaper one, like those over there?* (A clear Yes or No is not possible. Too complicated and convoluted.)

YES: *For the needs of my body at this point in time, is this brand of vitamin C the best in this store for me?* (Pins it down.)

Here are a few things to keep in mind as you compose the wording of your question:

Be Specific

It's important to be precise and concrete. A man once used a pendulum at the supermarket to ask, *Which one is the ripest watermelon?* When he cut it open at a picnic soon afterward, it was so ripe it was falling in on itself. "He did get the ripest one, but what he wanted was one that was the 'perfect ripeness for eating in two hours,'" says Leroy Bull.

Other examples:

NO: *Does my car need gas?* (A car always needs gas to run.)

NO: *Does my car have enough gas?* (Sure, it will start up fine, but . . .)

YES: *Does my car have enough gas to get me to my next destination?* (Now you're getting specific information.)

Break It Down

If the question is complicated, break it down into two or three questions that you ask one by one. Asking a string of questions is also a good idea if the issue has lots of elements or ramifications. "Chunking down" a complex matter in this way not only gives you more precise answers, but helps you think through a problem. You'll see more clearly what is really important to you, which psychologists say is key in sifting through choices.

NO: *Is this a good job they're offering me?* (Vague.)

YES: *In this job, will I make enough money to pay all my bills? Will the work be stimulating? Will I be able to easily handle the stress levels? Will my co-workers be supportive of me?* (More specific, allowing you to check one by one the different elements that matter to you.)

Avoid Colorful Phrases

Be sure that your question is free of lingo and colloquialisms. The words must be literal—as if you're talking to a young child or someone who speaks limited English—and not symbolic or metaphoric. Some examples:

NO: *Will this person my friends are fixing me up with be a hot date?* (He or she might have a fever or it might be a sweltering night.)

NO: *Is this person a good match for me?* ("Match" has many meanings: he or she could be wearing the same colors, or could be an equally skilled tennis player, or could light your fire!)

NO: *Will this date be the man/woman of my dreams?* (Which dreams? Past, present, future? A terrible date might well show up in your dreams the next night.)

YES: *Is it in my highest and best good to go on this date?* (The bottom line! And action-focused rather than predictive.)

Should You "Should"?

There's also the whole question of whether the word "should" is the best choice. I personally have used it with great success, as in: *Should I buy this pair of sunglasses? Should I go to my college newspaper reunion in Chicago?*

But for many people, the word "should" is too loaded, and they get much better results with such phrases as:

Is it in my best and highest good to buy this pair of sunglasses?

Is this the best pair of sunglasses for me to buy in this store?

Try different wordings to see which one works best for you.

Take Your Time

Especially in the beginning, for important questions, don't rush the process. "By spending time and mulling it over and forming the question so that it really reflects what you want to know—so it's not just a little throwout question—you open the pathway to getting a wise answer, wise guidance," says author Garnette Arledge.

As you're composing the question, be attentive to what pops into your head. It could be a picture, a word, a thought. Sometimes by following it, you'll go deeper into the core of what you're seeking.

Keep It Personal

Divining is a sacred method of personalized guidance, so to use it for idle questions outside your range of action *(Will the Mets win the World Series?)* or to inquire into someone else's business *(Is my neighbor having an affair with the Fed Ex carrier?)* will get you nowhere fast with whimsical and misleading answers. Likewise, asking lie-detector questions *(Is he telling me the truth?)* is fraught with peril. Betrayal is such a gut-level fear that getting a clear reading—especially if our teenager is involved—is virtually impossible. Questions you might ask:

Should I buy a ticket for the World Series?

Is there something inside me blocking my communication with my teenager? Is it _____? Is it _____?

Try a Different Tack

If you're getting muddy answers, recast the question or take a step back and see if maybe you're heading down the wrong track. Sometimes taking a 90- or 180-degree turn will give you what you're actually looking for. Be creative: that's part of the fun and the learning curve.

When I was preparing my house for rental, I needed to upgrade the silverware, but was stymied at Target because not one of the three dozen patterns drew me. I tried testing for which one I would be happiest with, and kept getting very strange answers. It took another store and more testing before I finally asked a better question: *Would I be happy with any of these choices?* Yes! I used the silverware only two hectic weeks, so my feelings toward it were totally irrelevant. In retrospect, I should have asked, *Which of these patterns should I buy to make my future renters happiest?*

Composing the question is an art in itself, and you'll get better and better at it over time. The learning process continues to unfold. People with decades of practice still happily report coming up with new and better wording all the time.

Asking the Question

The moment has arrived! In these instructions, "check" means to check for the answer by muscle-testing or pendling.

Do a Preliminary Check

To start off, do a check to make sure your neuromuscular circuit is strong and "online." Say:

Give me a Yes. (Check.)

Give me a No. (Check.)

(If muscle-testing) *Give me a Choice.* (Check.)

If you don't get a strong response, back off the divining for now and take a break: sip water (dehydration can throw off your electrical balance), take a nap, go for a walk.

Get Permission

Not all things are meant to be known at all times. Getting certain information may not be to your advantage, or you may not be ready to hear it, or it may be hidden for other reasons. If you proceed without asking permission, the answers may well be confusing, misleading, or not useful. Ask:

Do I have permission to ask this question? (Check.)

Or you can break it down into three parts to get more information:

- *Can I ask this question?* (Check.)
  Am I physically, mentally, emotionally, and spiritually able to ask the question and hear the answer now? For example, if you're exhausted, attached to a certain outcome, or feeling fearful, the answer may be No.

- *May I ask this question?* (Check.)
  Is it the right time, the right question? Is it my business and not someone else's?

- *Should I ask this question?* (Check.)
  Is it in my highest and best interest to know this answer now? For example, perhaps you should wait the situation out or use other means—research, intuition, asking advice of others—to come up with the answer.

If you get a No on any of these, wait a while, and if you find the answer doesn't come some other way—through a synchronicity, friend, or sudden inner knowing—ask again in an hour, a day, a week. A No could mean that you already know the answer intuitively, that events will proceed just fine without your active involvement, or that you should use some other means to come to a conclusion. Don't take it personally. Even some masters at kinesiology report getting permission only 80% of the time. You can also ask:

Do I need to ask this question?

Is this something I need to know?

These questions are useful for heading off divining that gets too mechanical or that arises out of restlessness or anxiety rather than real need. If you get a No, try sitting back and looking at events as they unfold, with the attitude of "I wonder what will happen now!"

Step Into an Attitude of Simple Curiosity

Attitude is all-important here. Curious, receptive, vulnerable, open: this is the ideal state in which to get information. Feel a sense of "On your mark, get set . . ."—as though you're poised waiting for the bell to ring at the starting line. Or imagine you're a child about to open a present, or a technician about to read an instrument panel. Let your curiosity grow stronger and brighter and more intense: "This is really exciting! What am I going to find out?"

"Lock In" the Question

Keep the question in your mind in sharp focus, with as little wavering as possible. It's like sending out the signal that brings in the radio station or TV channel that you need from the tens of thousands of choices on the bandwidth.

The more strongly and firmly you hold the question in your mind, the clearer the reception—and the answer. If you are distracted by commotion or your to-do list, sit up straight, take a deep breath, lock in on your target, and . . .

Ask Your Question!

Now is the time! For example:

Should I _____?

Is it best for me to _____?

Is it a positive thing for me to _____?

Is it in my highest and best good to_____?

You can also pose the question as a statement, if that feels intuitively better to you:

I should _____.

It is best for me to _____.

It is a positive thing for me to _____.

It is in my highest and best good to _____.

If you have options to sort through, such as a date, you can ask:

Should I do this on ____? ____? ____? ____? (For example, Should I do this on October 15? 16? 17? 18?)

Or, I should do this on ____, ____, ____, or _____.

Check each option to see which one gives you a Choice response with your circuit fingers or a Yes with your pendulum.

If you have a list to work your way through, you can ask: *Is it this one? This one? This one?*

If you are faced with a wide variety of choices, such as products in a store, you can systematically sort through things by mentally grouping objects together and then honing in on the selections. Looking for sunscreens, for example, you can ask: *I'm looking for the most effective sunscreen for myself. Counting from the top down, which shelf is it on? Looking at brands, how many brands from the left is it? Within that brand, how many bottles from the left is it?* Or if you're choosing paint colors, for example, you can hold a wheel of five hundred paint colors in your hand and ask: *I want to paint my bedroom wall the color that will make me happiest when I open my eyes in the morning. Which strip is it on? How far down from the top?*

You can also break down large units into smaller ones and check them one at a time. For instance, looking through the phone book for a lawyer or plumber, you can ask: *What page is it on? Which column? Which part of the column—top, middle, or bottom? How many names down from the top of that part?*

Because muscle-testing and pendling are so quick, it's easy to find your mind jumping ahead to question five, say, even as you're asking question four. Watch out for this! Your mind must be fully focused on four, otherwise—like a radio dial between stations—the "signals" will cross and you'll get interference and confusing answers.

EXERCISE
KEEP A DIVINING LOG

Start a journal to hone your question-asking ability and chart your divining sessions. Write a question, then edit and rewrite it until it is as simple and direct as possible. After you divine, record the answer, and, as events unfold, record the outcome. You'll get a sense of when and how your accuracy increases: for instance, when you test seriously rather than casually, when you're emotionally balanced rather than overloaded, when you're rested rather than exhausted.

STEP 5. RECEIVE THE ANSWER

Mysteriously, miraculously, astonishingly—the answer arrives.

For a moment or two, sit with it and let it sink in.

The reply may match your desires or not, but you may well get a feeling of rightness about it. "There's an inner sense that goes 'Bingo!' or 'Hole in one!'" says Gailann Greene. "There's an energy about it, a charge around it that makes it feel like it's got light rays of truth around it." Sometimes, of course, the feeling is attached to a sinking sensation that you're about to embark on an adventure you hadn't planned on.

Before you jump up and swing into action, take a slow, deep breath and go through the following steps.

Check Your Gut

Look inside to see how the answer received feels on a gut level. Be honest with yourself. Underneath the dismay or excitement, does it feel right? Does it "click"? Does it "fall in the slot"? Does it have a sense of inevitability about it, a feeling of the unfolding of destiny?

Getting this inner Yes! is absolutely key. Along with it might come a deep, profound silence, if only for a millisecond—and then your mind might get very noisy indeed. Getting answers we don't want is proof that divining is working: we're not overriding the delicate process with our desires or preconceived ideas. Time will show you why and how the answer benefits you. "The best answers can be ones that aren't logical, because then you know your rational mind didn't get in the way," says Leroy Bull. If we always get the answers we want, we must become a little suspicious of our divining.

But again, check your gut—that is what matters. Do not move forward unless it gives you the go-ahead. "The truth of a thing is the *feel* of it, not the *think* of it," goes one saying.[1]

"I am more times than not shocked at what comes up," says Darlene Van de Grift. "It's as though you're on a moving train and nothing supports you jumping off that train except for the inner knowing that, 'Oh my God, I know this guidance is right, I've got to leave this situation, I've got to do something different.' Whether it's due to ego or saving face or the energy that's involved, it's easier to just keep on going. My lesson is to listen to the truth when it is something I don't want to hear—and to do it."

On the other hand, does the guidance feel off? Not quite right? Somehow slipshod or out of sync? Listen to yourself carefully and trust your instincts. Although divining is about 90% accurate for dentist Buzzy Tischler, he says, "I can get fooled. But if it's a serious thing, I sense what's true and what's not true. It's hard to explain, but something inside says 'This is so' or 'This is not so.'"

You can train yourself to recognize the physical sensations in yourself that signal inner certainty: it might be dramatic, like a tingle up the spine or a grounded feeling in the gut, or it might be subtle, like a slight relaxing of the heart muscles. At a time when you get a sensation clear and strong, tell yourself, "This is what a right answer feels like." Feel fully how the energy moves in your body. In the future, this will help you find your way in divining and in daily life.

Verify If Necessary

If you're asking a major life-changing question, it's extremely wise to double-check and triple-check the reply. Even on minor questions, if the answer sets you back on your heels, you'll want to get confirmation that you haven't made a mistake. There are several ways to do this.

- Ask again. Scott Cunningham, author of *Divination for Beginners,* recommends asking a question three times if need be. Use different words, to make sure you haven't erred by using double meanings or loose language, or go at it from a different direction. It's a wise idea to put a three-time limit on your rechecking, lest it become obsessive.

- Verify the answer by asking the question with one of the other two tools, or by using one of the supplementary approaches in chapter 11, preferably after waiting a day or two.

- Ask the Divine to verify it in some other form, like synchronicity, a dream, or an inner shift.

- See what question arises in your mind—perhaps another option or question or a logistical detail. Ask it. For example: *Is there anything else I should know? That I should ask? Can you give me another option that will work just as well? Is it _____? Is it _____?* You can keep on dialoguing in this way until you have a good understanding of what you need to do next. You'll find more complete suggestions for dialoguing on page 177 in chapter 8.

- Ask, *Do I need more time before going ahead with this answer?* For instance, you may get a Yes about writing a book or moving elsewhere, but when you probe, you may not need to undertake it for several years.

- Blind-test by asking another person who divines to verify it.

- Sleep on it, or put it out of your mind for two or three days, and then see how you feel about it. Quite often, something will change internally without any conscious effort, and you'll feel ready to go ahead with the counsel. Also, sometimes dilemmas disappear on their own, and it can be important to listen to that voice telling you not to move on a decision just yet.

Be careful that you're not working hard to get a Yes instead of a No, or vice versa, because your desire for a different answer will eventually bring it your way, erroneously. "You've got to take it like it is—if it says No, it means No," says master dowser Joe Smith. "If you keep asking the same question, it will finally tell you Yes. Your subconscious will take over and say, 'If that's what he wants to hear, that's what we'll give him.'"

If you don't like the answer you get, "Just say 'Thank you very much' and do as you please," concurs Marty Cain. "I don't want a lie. I don't want it saying 'It's okay' just to make me happy. I want to know the truthful consequences of my actions, and then I get to choose what to do." For that reason, she doesn't try to wheedle an answer out of it—like a Yes to eat Ben & Jerry's. Instead, she'll bypass the dowsing and get the ice cream, or not.

Of course, the opposite dynamic might happen—you might be more than delighted because the answer is what you had hoped to hear! Again, do that gut check, to make sure you're on target. If so, wonderful—you're in the flow and on your way. But if you're suspicious that your desires overrode the process, you can ask a simple but key question: *Did I just engage in wishful divining?* If the answer is Yes, laugh and try again later.

Self-honesty is key to getting a sound answer to that question. Be sure you're quiet, connected, and neutral when you ask, and that you want the truth more than reassurance.

If your muscle-testing or pendling is confusing, contradictory, or balky, it may be because you're tired, dehydrated, unfocused, or trying too hard, among other factors. In appendix 1, you'll find a Divining Checklist that will help you troubleshoot any problem.

Give Thanks
You've asked, you've received. Now, for at least a moment, express your appreciation to the Divine. "There's a law of compensation in the Universe, so if you're asking something, you must give something in return," says Rick Jarow. "It's acknowledging the Source and honoring the fact that you're in partnership." This can take physical form, like a small bow or putting a flower on an altar. Or it can be a silent thank you, a deep sense of gratitude, a prayer, a silent song, a chant or Om, or the respectful intention to take the answer seriously. What's important is not the form but the sincere feeling. Infused with gratitude, you move out into the world with an overflowing heart that makes all things possible.

BLIND-TESTING TO BYPASS THE "ME FACTOR"

If you can't disengage from a strong emotion or a decided preference about a decision, like whether to phone your ex, you can blind-test to reduce the impact. You can also blind-test if you're concerned some subliminal preference might color your divining. When Sandi Ruelke looked through classified ads to find a Jack Russell terrier, she didn't pendle directly; instead, she numbered seven choices and then numbered seven 3" x 5" cards from one to seven. Then she turned the cards over, mixed them up, and pendled them for first and second choice. "A name, a word, a number—you can never tell what might influence you," she says.

Some ways to bypass the "me factor" are:

When Asking the Question

- On identical-looking pieces of paper, such as your business cards or playing cards, write *Yes, No,* and *?* (a question mark). Turn them over so you can't read them, mix them up, arrange them on a tabletop like spokes of a wheel, and with the question firmly in your mind, muscle-test or pendle them one by one. If the question mark comes up, it could mean that you don't have permission, the question is unclear or heads in the wrong direction, or it may not be the right procedure to use.

- Put one, two, and three (or more) dots on the back of business cards. Assign meanings in your mind depending on the question (for instance, one is Yes, two is No, three is Wait; one is Sony, two is Apple, three is Wait). Mix and divine for them as described above.

- If you're sorting through options, write the various choices on identical slips of paper (like Post-it notes), turn them over so you can't read them, shuffle and move them around until you forget which is which, and then divine them one by one.

- If you have a number of questions, write them out on a sheet of paper, and then in a random manner, assign letters to each, such as *D* to the first question, *A* to the second, *G* to the third. Cover it up or put it aside. Then muscle-test or pendle by verbally going from *A* to *G*, asking for a Yes or No and writing down the responses. Compare the results with your list.

To Verify an Answer

- Call a person who muscle-tests or pendles and run it past them to see if they get the same answer. You don't even have to tell them what the question is, since their opinion might affect the response. Just "lock in" on the question in your mind while they test it.

Leroy Bull often blind-tests for other dowsers: "They'll call me on the phone and say, 'I have ten choices. I've numbered them on this piece of paper from one through ten. Which is in my best interest?' And I just say to myself: 'One, two, three, four, five, six . . . ' I tell them, 'Number six. Good-bye.' Now, I don't know what they were talking about. I don't even know what the topic was."

Some dowsers, to double-check blind-testing by someone else, throw in a "fluff question"—something they know the answer to that doesn't really matter, like *Am I having chicken soup for dinner?*

- If you're blind-testing for yourself using cards or papers, ask a simple Yes/No question like, *Is today Tuesday?* to make sure you're on track.

- If you are fortunate enough to know a more experienced dowser (perhaps through the ASD), you can work with the person to both verify your answers and build your skills.

When dowsing teacher Anne Williams first learned to pendle, she recalls, "I didn't trust some of the answers I was getting, so I would write them down and then ask my dowsing teacher to check the answers for me. I told her I wasn't going to tell her the answers I had gotten because I didn't want to influence what she got. In this way, my dowsing became stronger, and I began to develop confidence that I was really getting some clear, accurate answers."

EXERCISE
CULTIVATING GRATITUDE

If you find it hard to feel gratitude in your life, taking simple steps can turn that around—with profound effects for well-being, studies show. Try this: each night for one week, write down five things that you're thankful for that happened during the day (for instance, the sight of someone smiling, no headache, hearing from an old friend). One study found that people who did this were significantly happier six months later than a control group. Or once a week for ten weeks, write down five things you're grateful for. This raised the "set point" of happiness for people by 25% and helped them to sleep more soundly and exercise more.[2] People who keep ongoing gratitude journals are ill less often, cope better with stress, and are less likely to be envious, greedy, or bitter, numerous studies show.[3]

Finally, Machaelle Small Wright has some wise words to say about muscle-testing, which apply equally well to pendling:

> *In teaching kinesiology, I have found that something interesting happens to some people when they are learning it. Every block, doubt, question, concern, and personal challenge they have, when faced head-on with something perceived as unconventional, comes right to the surface. It is as if the physical tool of kinesiology itself serves to bring to the surface all those hurdles. So they learn kinesiology right away and are using it well. Then, all of a sudden it is not working for them. When they tell me about it, I realize that the thing they do differently now that they didn't do at first is double-checking their answers—and rechecking, and*

*rechecking, and doing it again, and again. . . .
Each time the answers vary or the fingers get
mushy and they get definite maybes.*

*Well, again the issue is not the kinesiology.
The issue is really why they are suddenly doing
all this rechecking business. What has surfaced
for them are questions around trust in their own
ability, belief that such unconventional things
really do happen and are happening to them.
They have a sudden lack of self-confidence.*

*Again, the only way I know to get over
this hurdle is to defy it—keep testing. . . .
The successful results, in turn, give you confidence about your testing ability. The other
alternative is to succumb and stop developing
kinesiology. But that doesn't really accomplish
anything. So in cases like this, I suggest the
person keep testing,* stop double-checking,
*and take the plunge to go with the first test
result. Eventually, what action is taken
based on the first test result will verify the
accuracy of the test. As I've said, from this
your confidence builds. I firmly believe that
only clear personal experience and evidence
can get us through these kinds of blocks and
hurdles—and that means just continuing to
go on.*

EXERCISE
ASKING EVERYDAY QUESTIONS

For the next two weeks, practice by divining for the answers to everyday questions like what route to take to work and what entrée to order or cook for dinner, gradually building up to more important questions.

BUDDY UP!

When we're first learning to divine, it's a great help to feel supported. Although we can't necessarily expect our loved ones to back us in this venture, usually we can round up a willing friend to play alongside us. As you work your way through this book, the two of you can encourage each other, bounce ideas off each other, verify each other's findings, and have fun exploring new avenues. You might want to get together to practice, or attend a divining class or workshop together. If there's no one close to home, you can find a divining buddy at whattodobook.com.

One interesting thing you'll learn is how subjective—not objective—answers are, and how individualized they are to our needs. For example, if you blind-check your friend's findings on how she can resolve conflicts with her boss, you may find over time that your answers are more accurate, but she may still have to go through certain rugged experiences—including building up a high level of frustration—to produce a real, lasting shift in herself. Exploring these kinds of intricacies together will give you a deeper appreciation of how divining works and life unfolds.

Likewise, if you're with a friend or relative who opposes divining, it's wise not to show off! Because you are linked mentally and emotionally with them even as you act counter to their beliefs, you may encounter a subtle internal dissonance, which makes the signals fuzzy and your answers mushy. Especially when you start out, be tender and protective with your process; later, as your divining muscles strengthen, that won't be necessary. It's like the Indian parable of the young sapling that needs a fence encircling it to protect it from being eaten by wild animals. When it's older and stronger, the same animals gratefully find shade beneath it.

AND NOW . . . THE FUN BEGINS

As you follow the advice from your divining, you get to enjoy the unfolding of events in your life that come to fruition as you learn to trust your answers. You'll find occurrences lining up to support you in the most unexpected and unlikely ways. You'll get the sense of the pieces of the puzzle falling effortlessly together. Meaningful coincidences will come together and fortuitous events will happen, and you'll start to understand why the advice you received was the ideal path for you. This doesn't mean that it will necessarily be smooth, because sometimes the advice we take will transport us into our deepest emotional blocks, but we will emerge from that process with greater clarity and love and openness. We have to—because we now have a deal with the Divine. We are trusting it, and it must support us on our road to Ultimate Oneness. That is its job.

Over time and with proof, your trust in divining will build. But if you find your doubts growing instead of declining, it may be that whatever tool you're using—muscle-testing or pendling or the chits—is not the right tool for you, and you may want to try another. Or divining itself may not be the right spiritual path for you, and you may want to deepen your ability to access your intuition without a tool. Good books on that are listed in appendix 2.

Remember that once you know the basics, you can put your own fingerprints on divining. For instance, as you'll see, you can dialogue to get more information, you can ask the percent of benefit of one option over another, or you can explore other alternatives. You can even ask for another answer. Rick Jarow tells of a time when he consulted the *I Ching* about the best course of action for a fractious issue at his son's school. The *I Ching* advised him to do nothing: "I told the *I Ching* that's unacceptable, and I threw again." This time, it counseled him that if he were to do something, he should get other people on his side. "It turned out very well," he says. "I felt good about that as opposed to just accepting the verdict."

Some people choose not to follow advice because they want to learn the lessons involved or because they can't stop themselves from going in that direction, or don't want to. "Sometimes when I get a No, I just want to do it anyway and I feel good about doing it anyway—so that's what I do," says dancer Kathleen Donovan. "It's not my religion, like I have to do it." Or they decide to go another route. "There are some things you need to sort through in your head," says Darlene Van de Grift. "As much as I may trust muscle-testing and I will use it when I feel I need to, I don't want it to be in control of my whole life."

Don't forget, the choice is always yours on whether to follow the counsel. "If good common sense tells you the answer is really not the best thing for you to do right now, it's better to hold off on it—even if it's so you can clear the fear that stands in the way of your success," says Anne Williams.

Now that you know how to ask questions in a way that ensures useful results, you've completed the beginning course in divining. With the strategies you learn in the next chapter, you'll be able to fine-tune the process to get increasingly useful data from that great "library in the sky."

CHAPTER 7

THE NEXT LEVEL

HONING IN ON THE INFORMATION

Once you have the basic mechanics and five-step procedure down, you'll find that divining goes swiftly and smoothly. At this point, the following approaches may help you to hone in on information to make it more precise and useful, much as you would click repeatedly on a Google map to take it from a global level down to the street level. These techniques—which include using percentages to gauge how accurate and beneficial an approach is, engaging the alphabet, using charts to precisely target information, using maps to locate lost items, and adding more pendulum responses—can help you refine and clarify your answers. They can increase the accuracy, depth, and usefulness of the information you receive.

As you personalize your process, using any of these approaches is a matter of preference. Whether they work for you or not depends on your conditioning and mental patterns. For example, if you have the kind of rigorous mind that prizes precision, you'll enjoy making use of percentage scales. If you like to sort through things with little fuss as quickly as possible, you'll appreciate charts. If you like things pared down, you may skip the numbers but use the alphabet when you're searching for a word or destination. Try out the approaches and use what works. The most important thing is to keep your divining simple and fun by doing what feels right, natural, and useful to you.

WALK-THROUGH: WHAT HONING IN MIGHT LOOK LIKE

To see how honing in might work, let's go back to that imaginary vacation planning:

I'm just not sure about Montana. Lately I've really been wanting to be by the ocean. What is the percent of positivity for me taking my vacation on the Maine coast? 55%.

Can I raise that percent? Yes.

By booking a room on Monhegan Island? Yes.

By visiting my second cousins in Portland? No.

By mapping out exactly what I want to do? No.

By getting tickets for a whale-watching tour? Yes.

How high can I bring it? 76%.

What's the percent of positivity for me vacationing in Montana? 95%.

Okay, I guess I'll go with Montana. How many days should I spend river rafting? Nine.

Starting on what date? August 10.

What shall I do the last five days: Sightsee around Missoula? Trout fish? Backpack into the wilderness?

I'm only getting mushy Nos. Do I need to know this answer at this time? No.

Is it best to wait and see what happens? Yes.

Will it become clear to me on the raft trip what to do next? Yes.

Montana is bound to be crowded in late August—that makes me wonder about room reservations. What is the percent of probability that after August 19 I'll be able to find a hotel room or place to stay that I like at a reasonable price? 93%.

As you sit back and let it sink in—Montana? Okay, Montana!—more questions might naturally arise in your mind. We'll pick up this dialogue in the next chapter on advanced techniques.

RUNNING THROUGH THE NUMBERS: PERCENTAGES AND THE 1–10 SCALE

Percentages and the 1–10 scale are useful measurements for sharpening your divining findings; they can help you assess the relative accuracy, impact, value, and importance of your answers. For example, if you're lost and someone gives you road directions, it's useful to know if they're 40% or 100% correct. If you have back pain, you may decide to chance the side effects of a painkiller if it alleviates 70% of your symptoms but not if it eliminates only 15%. And choosing running shoes may be easier if, on a scale of 1–10, the Adidas get a 6 and the Nike an 8 in terms of long-term comfort.

Again, what matters is what works for you. You can ask these questions in ways that don't require percentages or numbers. For example:

Should I follow this person's directions?

Will this painkiller ease my back pain? Will it cause major side effects?

Which pair of shoes will be most comfortable a month from now?

But if you enjoy exactitude, numbers can be fun for you. And if you want to expand your range of inquiry, they can take you down some intriguing avenues.

Counting Off Using Muscle-Testing

Use the "Give me a choice" option when counting off. That involves going through a list, testing item by item, until your circuit fingers open (or close, depending on your calibration) on the answer. For instance, in the approaches on the following pages that use percentages, you would ask:

What percent is it? 10, 20, 30, 40, 50, 60, 70, 80, 90, 100.

A speedy variation is to "chunk it up" by combining numbers: *0–50, 50–70, 80, 90, 95, 100.*

You can refine it further. If you get, say, 70%, you can test: *70, 71, 72, 73, 74, 75, 76, 77, 78, 79.*

The 1–10 scale is a variation on percentages that may work better for you. You can assess just about anything on the 1–10 scale, with 1 being low and 10 being high: degree of happiness, stress, health, compatibility, usefulness, to name just a few. (You can also make 1 high and 10 low, if that feels intuitively right.)

On a 1–10 scale, how healthy would bacon and eggs be for me this morning?

On a 1–10 scale, how much stress will I have if I take that committee position?

On a 1–10 scale, how much benefit will I receive from taking that committee position?

On a 1–10 scale, how much wear will I get out of this shirt?

On a 1–10 scale, how compatible am I with him/her mentally? Emotionally? Physically? Spiritually?

Then you simply muscle-test up the scale, until you land on the right number: *1, 2, 3, 4, 5, 6, 7, 8, 9, 10.*

Counting Off Using Pendling

Most commonly, people using a pendulum will pinpoint numbers by counting swings. Because a swing has a certain momentum, you can count very slowly and await each answer. Or you can count faster, narrow it down to a certain range, and then go back to those numbers and pendle slowly for each one. For example: *1, 2, 3, 4* (pendulum starts moving), *5, 6* (pendulum stops), *7, 8, 9, 10.* And then ask: *Is it 4? 5? 6?*

Pendlers also often use a pie-shaped chart. With the point of the pendulum hanging over the base of the chart, hold the question in your mind and watch where the pendulum swings (see figure 8, page 148).

Since the chart is not that portable, two other close-at-hand approaches when you're pendling on the fly are to pendle your watch face (assuming it's not digital) or your

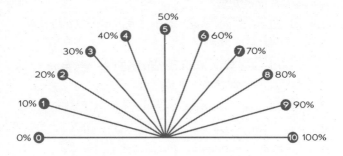

Figure 8: Counting chart

hand. Some people have a small pendulum on their key chain (available from the ASD bookstore) that they can use for purposes like this without attracting too much curiosity.

With a watch, the 12 stands for the zero point; 11 is a Neutral, indicating it's not the right approach or timing, or the question should be asked some other way. An advantage to the watch is that it also gives you a more precise number: a pendulum pointing midway between 3 and 4 is easy to interpret as 35%, for example (see figure 9).

The palm of the non-pendulum-holding hand is also easy to use. Ask the question, then hold the pendulum over the center of your palm and watch how it swings. The fingers indicate the odd numbers, with the thumb standing for 1 or 10%; the space between them indicates the even numbers. If after getting an answer, say 70%, you

 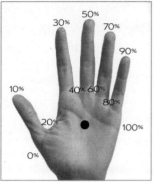

Figure 9: Watch chart   Figure 10: Hand chart

want it to be more specific, ask it to swing again toward the second digit—2 for 72%, 8 for 78% (see figure 10).

With this numbering system, you can now get at some very specific information.

Percent of Accuracy

This is a useful question to ask in the very beginning of a divining session, after you get permission to test, or midway through if the subject changes course or you start getting inconsistent answers: *What percent of accuracy am I getting?*

Then run through the numbers. If your accuracy is not at least 90%—and hopefully 100%—it is wise to take a break and come back to it later. Or you can probe the reason by asking, *Is the cause of the inaccuracy on the mental level? Emotional? Physical? Spiritual?*

Then you can get specifics, perhaps using the Divining Checklist in appendix 1 to sort through the possibilities. For example, if it's on the mental level, you can ask:

Is the question unclear?
Did I lose my focus during the questioning?
Did I skip the step of asking permission?
Do I really need the information?

Once you get a response, you can make internal adjustments, perhaps by looking up the proposed solution, until you raise it to 100%.

Sometimes I forget to ask about accuracy initially and am reminded by a few puzzling answers—only to find that I'm testing at 60% accuracy. I should have gone for a walk instead! I've also learned to be double sure I'm quiet, connected, and neutral in asking the accuracy question. If I am intent on proving my propitious findings correct rather than simply being open and curious, it can easily turn into wishful divining, which is no help at all.

Percent of Positivity or Benefit

This approach is useful for burrowing deeper into information in a way that allows you to make changes to affect an outcome. If you get a Yes on a proposed course of action—say, taking a workshop or dropping in on a friend—you can further refine the information by asking, *What is the percent of positivity?* Or, *What is the percent of benefit?* As indicated earlier, you then go up through the scale, gently testing each choice until you hit the right number and your fingers open (or close, if that is your calibration response): *10, 20, 30, 40, 50, 60, 70, 80, 90, 100.* Or, *0–50, 50–70, 80, 90, 95, 100.*

This question allows you to weigh your answers so you can better assess their value. For example, 100% of positivity is a full-steam-ahead type of answer; 50% may give you more pause, and more sense of choice.

If you find this approach useful, you can determine what percent of positivity is enough for you to go ahead with an action. Some of my friends will only proceed if it is at least 80% or even 90%.

You can continue muscle-testing or pendling to explore ways to raise the percent by taking certain actions or making changes in yourself. You can ask questions like, *Can I do something to improve this percentage?* (Then ask about certain options as they occur to you.) Or, *Is there some change I can make in myself to improve this percentage? Is it on the spiritual, mental, emotional, or physical level?* (Ask about options.)

Here is how it works for my friend Barbara Lubow. When she was going through a divorce and looking for a new place to live, she muscle-tested her way through the "apartment for rent" classified ads and found one that tested at 100% positivity. But she couldn't get the owner on the phone. Because she was in action mode, she arranged to look at a few apartments that tested at 70% and 50%, as long as the owner was amiable and it happened easily. "I would never take an apartment that came up 50%, but I wanted to know for myself, what does a 50% look like?—and it made me very grateful for what was 100% when I finally saw it," she says. "I just knew that I was going to get the apartment that tested 100%—not that it's guaranteed, but more often than not, if something tests out to be 100%, that's the best course and the green light is on."

She did in fact take that apartment, and when she went shopping to furnish it, she saw a hope chest that only tested at 60%. She tested to see if she could bring it up to a 90% if she painted, covered, or upholstered it, and got a Yes, so she bought it. Looking at a couch, she doubted her aesthetic judgment, so she thought of a friend with good taste and asked, *Would she like it?* "It doesn't speak well for me wondering how another person would view it, but the fact that testing can even do that is mind-boggling," she says with a laugh.

This, again, is your own play of consciousness, and you can design it however works best for you. Says Barbara: "If a person always goes ahead when they get a Yes, without asking about any percentage, the Divine will know that when it gives a Yes, that is going to mean action for that person. In my case, when I get a Yes, it has to give me a high percentage to get me to act. It all depends on how you set it up."

Some people take the percent of benefit a step further, muscle-testing beyond 100% to 200%, 300%, 400%, 500%, infinity. Logically, of course, this doesn't work—100% positive is as good as it gets on a percentage scale—but they use it to discover just how "over-the-top" a positive benefit can be. Probably life changing, with those numbers!

Percent of Possibility and Probability

The purpose of divining is not fortune-telling, yet it's tempting—since we now can access vast realms of information—to ask what's going to happen next. There is a way to do this that is not idle crystal-gazing; rather, it is a practical application you can use for growth and decision-making. Faced with something you would like to achieve or something you'd like to avoid, you can ask these twin questions:

What is the percent of possibility?
What is the percent of probability?

Possibility is the outside limit, probability the inside limit. As one saying goes, "It's possible, but not probable." Together they give you a range, like a weather forecaster saying that the chances of rain tomorrow are between 30% and 70%. For instance, if you're aiming for a promotion, it may be 80% possible but only 35% probable. These numbers give you something to work with: you can probe with more questions to learn what is standing between you and the full possibility, such as a mistaken belief or emotional block.

For example, you can ask if there are ways you are unconsciously blocking that promotion, and then muscle-test or pendle the levels of yourself: physical, emotional, mental, spiritual (explained in more detail in the next section). As you check out the different possibilities, explanations will come into your mind and hidden dynamics may well surface. For example, you may find that deep down, you don't really believe you can handle the new responsibilities, and perhaps that is linked to a childhood fear of failure and punishment. Or the process may clarify your doubts: you fear that the promotion will require too much physical stamina or time away from your children, or will keep you at a company you'd rather leave. Just having the information out of your unconscious and on the table, so to speak, changes the dynamics and allows you to either change your mind about what you want or to make mental and emotional adjustments that make your desired outcome more likely.

Be cautious, though. Venturing into the future even in this practical way is tricky, because as events play out in the lives of everyone concerned, the future and those percentages can change in a split second. And the further off in time something is, the greater the chance that things will shift. "You've got to be fluid and free enough to not get locked into the outcome, because what may be really important is what you learn heading down that path," says Darlene Van de Grift—a lesson *The Wizard of Oz* so aptly taught.

Levels of Self

In life, situations confront us to make us grow and expand in the various levels or dimensions of ourselves: physical, emotional, mental, spiritual. Often, we can get helpful direction by asking questions like this, and muscle-testing or pendling after each option, *Is this lesson on the physical, emotional, mental, or spiritual level?* There's a fifth possibility as well, which can be called X-factor: it means an outside person, circumstance, dynamic, or event beyond our control. For example, *Is the cause of this obstacle primarily physical, emotional, mental, spiritual, or X-factor?*

The answer can help you figure out the best approach. For example, if you're not getting the go-ahead on a house you're thinking of buying, you may ask more questions with divining and learn that it is because of a physical factor like radon in the basement; an emotional factor like a hostile next-door neighbor; a mental factor like a poor understanding of the finances involved; a spiritual factor like first having to finish up a karmic pattern involving your current house; or an X-factor like the deed not being fully legal. Once you've addressed the block, it's possible that you'll get clear sailing with the house.

The Alphabet

If you're searching for a word during divining—for instance, to identify an emotion or the name of a person—you can muscle-test through the alphabet to find the first letter, the second, and so on. You can test letter by letter—*A, B, C, D, E, F*—or chunk it up by asking, *Is it between A and F? G and L? M and R? S and Z?* and then narrowing it down: *G, H, I, J, K, L.*

If you are pendling, you can use a chart (see figure 11, page 156). Specify to the pendulum that you want a strong, clear swing.

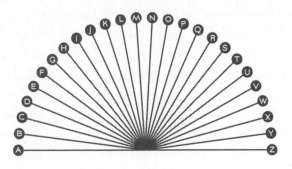

Figure 11: Alphabet chart

Jenny used this technique to communicate with a cat that appeared on the doorstep of her country home. Her husband shooed it away, saying, "I only want one cat!" But it kept coming back. Jenny muscle-tested to ask it its name. The answer: Ceone. See One! "It was saying, if you don't want two cats, just see one and it's not a problem," she laughs. The cat stayed.

ZEROING IN WITH PENDLING CHARTS

As you've seen, a chart allows you to zoom in on complex information with precision and efficiency. A chart pre-organizes the options for you so you can find out rapidly what you need to know. Although you can muscle-test your way through charts, it's somewhat awkward: they're specifically designed for pendling, and it is one application that you may want to adopt even if pendling is not your primary tool.

A pendling chart is typically pie-shaped or half-pie-shaped with options arranged at the end of the rays emanating from the center. When you hold the pendulum over the center and focus on a question, it swings toward the answer. It's that simple.

Some of the first published charts were produced by Anne Williams, a well-known New York City dowser, in 1979. "I didn't want to be stuck with just Yesses and Noes and not be able to find out the whys and wherefores," she says. Her book, *The Pendulum Book of Charts,* has charts for identifying your mood, picking a good color, and assessing nutrient levels. Today, thick spiral-bound books are easily available from many experts that can help you precisely identify just about every problem or need, from herbs to car repair to career options.

For a comprehensive, all-purpose chart, you can down-load a multipurpose form by long-time dowser Walt Woods at lettertorobin.org. The chart, which is complicated enough to resemble a vehicle control panel, indicates degrees of Yes and No, percentages, an incomplete question, and the need to change to a different subject, among other responses.

Charts can also be handmade and extremely simple, like the one on page 158. Although composed of just two lines and three words, it allows not just a Yes and No, but a gradient to show you the degree of Yes or No, depending on the degree of swing (see figure 12).

Charts can be easily sketched out for almost anything—food, for example. Is wheat good or bad for you?

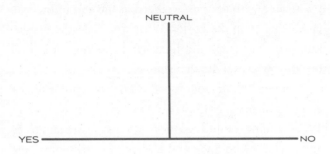

Figure 12: Yes/No chart

What about dairy? Meat? Eggplant? There are so many food theories that it's almost impossible to sort your way through them logically, but this scale can help you assess whether a food is good or bad for you at this point in time. You can also use it to determine if a food is best prepared boiled, steamed, fried, or raw (see figure 13).

In this chart, the meanings are:

Daily: Indulge! This food is really good for you.

Often: Eat two to three times a week.

Occasionally: Eat no more than once a week.

Rarely: Nibble small amounts on rare occasions.

Never: Do your body a favor and do not eat this food at all.

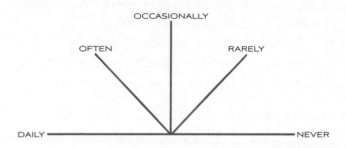

Figure 13: Food chart

As you can see, making your own chart is as easy as, well, pie. For example, for his senior-year project as a college forestry student, Scot Foxx pendled prescriptions for land management using his own set of technical charts, with such options as regeneration, harvest, shelter-wood, patch-cutting, multi-aging, and even-aging. He didn't have to walk the land, he found: the pendling worked equally well with an aerial photo. "Landowners have goals and objectives they want their land managed toward, but I also believe those stands of trees and the earth have their own opinion as to what they want done, and the pendulum is a way to bring it all together," he says.

You don't even need paper and pencil to make a chart. Once, when Tom Ruelke was working at a local recycling center, he drew a curved arc in the dirt with a stick and used a window weight on a chain as a pendulum. He was trying to determine whether at least seven tons of aluminum were in the aluminum pile—the minimum weight for it to be hauled away. His pendling said 14 tons; the pickup driver came and weighed it on a scale at 14.3 tons.

You can also muscle-test your way through a chart by focusing on each option using the "Give me a choice" wording, but it's far easier to simply pendle.

IF YOU'RE OVERUSING DIVINING . . .

Keep in mind that, like everything else in life, it's possible to overdo divining. As you learn these techniques, it can be fun and useful to divine on many things to build your skills. If you enjoy it and you're getting good, accurate answers, no problem! But as time goes on, if you start to get an uneasy feeling that you're getting obsessive with it, or if you're racing through the process, or if your answers are getting inconsistent, there's a very simple solution.

Take three deep breaths before any muscle-testing or pendling and ask yourself, "Do I need to divine for this? Do I actually need to know this information at this time?" Wait for the answer to arrive intuitively, as an inner knowing.

Another approach is to go "cold turkey" by stopping all divining for a few days or weeks, and then starting it again slowly and gradually.

Your tools may give you a clue that it's time for time off: your muscle-testing fingers might get sore, or your pendulum might do a disappearing act. When Tanya Tkach of

Quebec, Canada, started pendling, she recalls, "I went crazy with it. I was using it with everything: food, gardening, my dogs, my decorations, clothes, colors. I just thought it was great. But then what started to happen was that I would lose my pendulums. They would break in my hand. They would crack. They would fall. They would disappear. I'd say, 'I know I put my pendulum on my table—now where could it be?' The message I was getting was, 'You don't need it at this time. Use your intuition instead.'"

MAP-DOWSING

Dowsing over maps is a simple but practical application of pendling that can yield mind-boggling information. It is used to pinpoint geographic locations for something you want to find. It could be something lost, like a piece of jewelry, a pet, or a person, or it could be prospecting for the best place for your next vacation or home.

The basic procedure is simple. On a table, spread out a map, the more detailed the better. After going through the pendling preliminaries, hold your lost or desired object firmly in mind. Take a ruler or straightedge and slowly slide it up the page horizontally with your left hand while holding your pendulum with your right. When it gives you a strong Yes, draw a line across the page. Then slide the ruler down the page to see if that same spot elicits the Yes response; if so, that verifies it. Then slide the ruler across the page vertically, from left to right; when the Yes arrives, draw another line. Verify it by moving the ruler from right to left. Where the two lines intersect is the place to go look. Another technique is to put your finger on different spots on the map, pendling for a Yes response.

A dowser in the Adirondacks used the ruler technique to help police locate two missing men who had vanished in midwinter in a pickup truck after buying beer—a case reported on the TV program *Strange but True*. The two lines intersected in the middle of Lake George. The police took the dowser out on a boat, and he dowsed with a forked stick for the exact spot to drop the anchor. It landed in the flatbed of the truck, forty-eight feet below, an extremely long shot considering that the lake is two miles wide and thirty-two miles long. (Apparently the men had been inebriated and driving the truck on the frozen lake.)

Although it may never be your job to find a lost person, if you're asked to do so, "Ask the spirit of the person first if they want to be found," advises Marta Smith. When she and her husband Joe pendled that question about one missing man, they got back a vehement No. "No wonder," sniffed his brother. "He stole some money from me!"

To find a lost object, you can pendle a map or floor plan of a house. By asking how far up from the ground an object is, you'll know whether it's on the floor or in a cabinet.

Lost pets are a particular challenge because they're constantly on the move. Instead of asking where they are, it's best to ask where they will be at a certain point in time when you can intersect with them. And they, too, may not want to be found. Dogs often run at their owner's call, but cats tend to hide.

REFINING YOUR PENDULUM SWINGS

If you would like to further refine your pendulum use, you can use two more swings that give you more immediate feedback than merely the Neutral response. Although you can get the same information by asking certain questions, these swings are an efficient shortcut. They are:

Re-start

This means that the question itself is not quite right, and you should try again with different wording, a different approach, or switch to a different subject entirely.

Ask, "Please show me a Re-start." Watch how it moves. If you are using the Directing approach, choose a direction you want it to swing for this response and mentally say, "This is what a Re-start looks like."

Not Now

This means the information is not available, or it's not the right time for you to receive it.

Ask, "Please show me a Not Now" or direct it, "This is what a Not Now looks like."

Run the pendulum through its paces with the following questions:

Re-start

Is my hair blond, brown, green, black, or purple? (Too many
choices, a bad question.)

*Is today a good day or a bad day to go sailing, skiing,
bungee-jumping or sky-diving?* (Vague, wordy, too
many choices.)

Not Now

Will you show me something I'm not supposed to know yet?

*Will you show me something for which the information is
not yet available?*

EXERCISE
HONING IN

For four weeks, systematically experiment your way
through each of these approaches to see which ones are
useful to you. You might start with something simple, like
a movie or restaurant choice, divining for the percentage
of benefit of various choices, asking which choice is best
for various aspects of self, what day and time is best, and
the probability of getting a seat.

CHAPTER 8

ADVANCED TECHNIQUES

ASKING WIDER AND DEEPER QUESTIONS

One of the delights of divining is exploring the universe of opportunities that it offers. Its uses for decision-making, self-growth, and spiritual expansion are endless. Divining will take you any place you're willing to go. And because it accesses the expansive unconscious, you'll discover creative suggestions and solutions that the careful conscious mind is hard-pressed to deliver.

Laying the groundwork is key, and you've done that by nailing down the basics and learning how to hone in on information to make it more precise and useful. In this advanced chapter, you'll learn how to widen the scope of your divining with open-ended queries and with pointed questions on a wide range of topics. And you'll see how to drill deeper into divining with an interactive process called dialoguing, which will allow you to get to the heart of complex personal issues and decision-making dilemmas.

Pick and choose as you like to find what works for you. Everything, of course, is optional—even divining itself!

WALK-THROUGH: WHAT ADVANCED TECHNIQUES MIGHT LOOK LIKE

Here is how you can use the advanced techniques in this chapter to dive deeper into the factors affecting a choice. In our scenario, you're Montana-bound for this vacation, but some questions are surfacing.

I don't know why, but when I think about Montana, I feel a little queasy. Is there something else I need to know about this trip? Yes.

Is it on the spiritual level? No.

Mental? No.

Emotional? Yes.

Physical? No.

X-factor? No.

Hmm, emotional. Does it involve anger? No. *Fear?* Yes.

Of air travel? No.

Of water? No.

Of being away from my job so long when someone else wants it? No.

Of getting thrown out of the raft and hitting my head on rocks? Yes.

Yeah, the thought of that makes me anxious. What is the possibility of that happening? 1%.

I guess I can live with that. But then where does this fear come from—my childhood? Yes.

How old was I? (Counting up.) Four.

Was that when I hit my head on the bottom of the pool? Yes.

Is that the origin of my fear? Yes.

Now that I know it consciously, is the fear reduced? Yes.
　　How much? 25%.

Is it possible to reduce it more? Yes.

*Is there a type of therapy or bodywork that would work
　　quickly?* Yes.

*Is it EMDR (Eye Movement Desensitization and
　　Reprocessing)?* No.

Cognitive? No.

Hypnotherapy? Yes.

How many sessions will it take to get over it? Three.

Can I get good results with someone locally? Yes.

*Can I easily find the name of the best person to go to in the
　　phone book?* No.

On the web? Yes.

By looking through hypnotherapy sites? Yes.

What letter does their last name start with? T.

Is it a woman or a man? Man.

*How much will the fear be reduced when it is
　　completed?* 90%.

About how much will it cost? $200.

*That's more than I want to spend. What if I just go ahead
　　and go—will the fear go away on its own once I am on
　　a raft?* Yes.

In how many days? Three.

Okay, I'm going to sit on this decision a few days. Is there anything I can do before going to minimize the actual risks of hitting my head? Yes.

Should I buy my own helmet? Yes.

Can I find the best choice in a local store? Yes.

Which store—Toys R' Us? No. *Target?* No. *REI?* Yes.

Pack your gear—you're ready for an adventure! Of course, you could decide to shuck it and go to the Maine coast where—who knows—you might eat lots of delectable lobster while getting rained on a lot. But if you follow through on Montana, odds are high that events will unfold harmoniously in ways that delight and awe you, giving you a sense of moving in concert with destiny: you might meet someone on the raft who will change your life, or have a mystical experience under a starry sky, or enfolded by the towering Beartooth Peaks, find the inner resolve to make a major life shift.

GOING WIDER WITH LINES OF QUESTIONING

Questions are key to divining, and we can widen our scope—and make life adventuresome—by asking open-ended ones that swing the door wide for guidance. We can also widen our scope, and make life efficient, by asking pointed questions on a wide range of everyday choices, such as food, finances, clothing purchases, workshops, and choosing an expert. To help inspire your creative process, here are some common lines of questioning. With time and experimentation, you can develop even better ones.

Open-Ended Questions

What do I need to do next? Is it___? Is it ___?

Is there something I need to be aware of now? On what level is it: physical, emotional, mental, spiritual, X-factor?

Is there something blocking me? If so, where? When?

Is there something I'm overlooking? On what level is it? Is it___? Is it ___?

Sometimes, without even realizing it, we limit ourselves by the very questions we pose. For example, you might be divining carefully on what new car to buy and what dealer to buy it from, but because the question is focused in that way, you won't receive the guidance that a cash-strapped neighbor is about to sell his late-model car at a very good price. By asking an open-ended question—for example, *Is there something I need to be aware of now?*—you create the opportunity for valuable information to flow in from unexpected quarters.

You can use questions like the ones above when you're working through a decision. You can also use them as a check-in with the Divine during the course of the day. By directing your attention where it needs to go, these questions streamline your choices and discourage aimless detours.

Pointed Questions

By being both precise and imaginative, you can garner all kinds of valuable tips from the Divine—and have fun making choices that might ordinarily be run-of-the-mill or stressful.

Food

Is this dish healthy for me? What is the percent of benefit?

On a scale of 1–10, what is the life force in this food?

(In a restaurant) *Which entrée will be the healthiest choice for me? Will taste best to me? Will be both tasty and healthy?*

(In your kitchen) *What ingredients should I put in this dish? What spices?*

(In a bookstore) *Which of these diet books will help me lose weight in a healthy way? Of these, which diet will I be able to stick to most easily?*

To be honest, we pretty much know what is good to eat, starting with lots of fruits and vegetables, but because it's so easy to find a recent industry-funded study proving that, say, Oreos are chock-full of antioxidants, we have an excuse to go astray. The answers to these questions cut through the info-clutter and give voice to our deeper impulse to do good by our body.

Supplements

(In a store) *Does my body need this vitamin/mineral/supplement in this specific form? What is the percent of benefit?*

*I am looking for a vitamin C that is easily absorbed by my
body and good value for the price. Which of these is my
best choice?*

*For the specific needs of my body at this point in time,
which of these brands of vitamin C is the best choice in
this store for me?*

Keeping on top of the research on supplements can be
a full-time job, and because the field is swirling with
controversy from pro-and-con special interests, it's easy
to be misled. Even if a supplement proves itself in a well-
designed clinical study, it may not be what you need for
your own unique body. Testing with questions like these
helps you cut through this thicket.

(At home) *Does my body need this vitamin/mineral/
supplement today? In what dosage?*

You can line up your bottles of supplements and test them
on a daily or weekly basis to see if each one is what your
body needs in the moment. In the same way, you can test
essential oils and Bach Flower Remedies to address emotional blocks or expand your awareness.

Finances

*Which stock or fund will give me the best return on my
investment?*

Should I sell this stock right now? How many shares?

Is this stock in a company aligned with my values?

Retired farmer Joe Smith of Johnson, Nebraska, picks stocks by going down the New York Stock Exchange list on the Internet with his pendulum. He writes down the top ten and brings the list to his wife, Marta. She uses her pendulum to pick the top one or two, then they pendle for the number of shares to buy. "I know little about the companies and my wife knows nothing, but we average a 29–30% annual rate of return on our portfolio," he says. Once they bought 200 shares in Applied Materials, Inc. for $24, which they sold six weeks later—again using the pendulum—for $50. But, he cautions, it may not work for everyone: "We dowse for need, not greed—if it's 'Gimme, gimme, gimme,' it doesn't work."

You can also muscle-test or pendle financial advice books to find the page you need to read. It's best to double-check with a financial adviser, of course. Test to find one who will act in your "highest and best interest."

Choosing Experts

Which of these [doctors, lawyers, dentists, plumbers, psychologists, mechanics, exterminators, contractors] is highly competent and will work for my highest good?

In the phone book, muscle-test or pendle each name. If there are many choices, chunk it up by first divining each column, then mentally dividing it into thirds and divining again, and then divining name by name. You can also include other criteria: that a doctor be open to acupuncture, for example, or that an exterminator use nontoxic sprays—information to verify with a phone call. You might even want to include that the doctor or dentist use muscle-testing or dowsing; it might save you some money. Dentist Buzzy Tischler of Woodstock, New York, uses a pendulum on people to assess the effect of mercury fillings. "I know mercury is a major poison, but I test everybody—and there are people who have amalgam fillings in their mouths and their bodies say it's all right," he says. "I have no idea why, but I won't take the fillings out."

Travel

What date should I leave on this trip? What date should I return?

What days should I spend in this place? That place?

Should we stay in an airport hotel? A historic hotel? A B&B? On this list, at what hotel is it in our best and highest good to stay?

Which is the best campsite for tonight?

Which restaurant on this street will give us the tastiest meal at a cost we can afford?

Which route shall I drive? Which exit shall I take for dinner?

When you're in new territory and in an exploring mode, you can rely on guidebooks and travel websites—perhaps outdated and with opinions not necessarily to your taste—or you can try out muscle-testing or pendling. The last option will give you more twists, turns, and unexpected delights. Once a friend and I were driving through New York State to Montreal, and we kept muscle-testing for the exit for lunch. It got later and later, and finally, about 3 p.m., we got a Yes. We ended up driving five minutes east into one of the prettiest little towns we had ever seen, right on Lake Champlain. We felt like we had stepped back in time fifty years, even to the chocolate malts we guzzled and the refreshing swim in the clear waters. Later, we read raves about Westport, New York, in a guidebook, but it was even more fun to stumble on it on our own, so to speak.

Shopping

(Clothes) *Which of these will fit me well? Be comfortable? Last a long time? Look good to my sweetheart?*

(Books) *Is it for my highest good to buy a book here today? What section is it in? What shelf? How far from the end?*

(Store location) *I want to buy a white stylish-looking toaster that holds extrawide bread and is energy efficient. Is it available? Which store will I find it in: JC Penney? Walmart? Costco?*

Some people know exactly what they want in a store and head straight to it. If that's not you, questions like those above can be helpful. If you're clothes shopping, hold your criteria in your mind and go down the rack muscle-testing or pendling. Or intuitively preselect three or four items and test each item for each of the criteria. Do be sure to try the selection on, of course! You can also save time and gas money by knowing in advance what store to head to. Because shopping can make the mind spin with desires, be sure you're quiet, centered, and calm throughout the divining process, and be prepared for some unusual purchases that bring out new aspects of yourself!

Purchase Options

Should I get this add-on?

Do I need this option?

What is the percent of benefit of this option?

When Tom and Sandi Ruelke bought a truck, the salesman offered them add-ons at a price, from a special undercoat to fancy speaker systems. They simply pendled their way through the list, getting straightforward Yesses and Noes.

How many do I need?

Will this fit in the space available?

You can also divine for quantity, timing, and other factors that affect your purchase. Shortly before my seventeen-month trip to India, I was buying huge plastic bins at Home Depot so I could store possessions in my neighbor's barn. Time was of the essence, and I had no clue how many would fit in my Hyundai Sonata or how many I actually needed. I muscle-tested: fifteen. The stack towered over my head on the dolly, but when I wedged the bins into the trunk, backseat, and front passenger seat, they fit perfectly, and there wasn't room for even one more. Of course, it turned out I needed them all.

The Marketplace of Ideas

Which of the courses in this catalogue is it in my best and highest good to take?

Which of these meditation techniques is the best one for me at this point in time?

At this conference, which speakers should I go hear?

Which form of therapy [cognitive, behavioral, Jungian, Freudian, EMDR] will be most useful for me in dealing with _____ issue? What is the percent of benefit?

Which of these schools of yoga is the best one for me physically and spiritually: Hatha, Ashtanga, Bikram, Vinyasa, Kundalini, Iyengar? Which teacher at this yoga center should I sign up with?

Which book in this store/library will teach me what I need to know next on my spiritual path?

Is it in my best and highest good to go listen to this spiritual teacher? What is the percent of benefit?

We are fortunate to live in a time when we have a world of options at our fingertips for mental exploration, self-healing, and spiritual expansion. The range of choices is so dazzling that it's easy to get sidetracked or misdirected. Questions like these streamline our journey and keep us on target, often by pointing to surprising choices that turn out to be just what we need. It's also important not to get rigid about the answer. We may be pointed toward a certain type of yoga or meditation, but it may be not so much a lifetime practice as a step on the way to another teacher or spiritual practice.

GOING DEEPER WITH DIALOGUING

You can use divining to get simple guidance, a Yes to this, a No to that. But it has the potential to be much more—an at-your-side mentor or guru whom you can bounce things off of to gain a deeper understanding of your situation and your choices. "Dialoguing is a way to unblock your discourse with the Universe so that it can help you like a therapist would," says San Francisco psychologist Harvey Schwartz, PhD. "You have to work at it, but when you do, creative new thoughts and intuitions come, and by the end of the conversation, you have a much more settled feeling about the decision you're making."

The following sections detail three uses of dialoguing, to give you a small idea of the range of possibilities:

- Sorting through a major decision

- Changing your behavior patterns

- Exploring obstacles and unwanted Noes

On your own, if it is your bent, you'll easily discover more ways to dialogue using muscle-testing or pendling. The only limitation to divining, after all, is our preconception of what's possible.

Sorting Through a Major Decision

Social scientists who study decision-making often urge a strategy called "weighted adding." This involves figuring out which factors are important to consider (for a vacation, it might be cost, travel time, weather, swimming opportunities, the availability of Lindt's 70% cocoa bars, etc.); how important they are relative to each other (cost might beat out Lindt's); how each choice compares (Maine might be hours away by car, Montana a day away by plane; Maine has the ocean, Montana rivers); and then soberly making a choice by evaluating which one comes out on top for the most important considerations. Of course, even for the most rational of us, life doesn't often work this way: we don't have all the information we need, we forget to include what's really important and overvalue what doesn't matter, and we can't predict many unknowables like weather. "We rarely do it and even if we try, we are not very good at it," writes Dutch psychologist Ap Dijksterhuis.

Again, it's just too much for the conscious mind to process—but this is an intriguing place for us to have fun by enrolling the unconscious mind, which, with the aid of divining, can hopscotch through the variables. Let's say, for instance, that you're torn between staying in the bustling city where you've lived for ten years or moving to a house on a quiet mountain road. You can start the dialogue by making a specific list of things that are important to you, such as:

Making more than enough money to pay my bills

Work that satisfies and stretches me

Spending time with my family

Good schools for my children

A sunny, spacious home

Easy access to biking trails

Top-notch music concerts

Lots of like-minded people, especially in the martial arts

A spiritual/religious community that I feel at home in

A gym with aerobics classes and weights

First-class medical care within an hour's travel time

As you make the list, take your time. Watch to see what images come into your mind. Think of the different levels of being—physical, emotional, mental, spiritual—and make sure all are covered. To make sure you're not overlooking something, ask:

Is there anything else that is important to me now?
Is it___? ___?
Is there anything else that might be important in the future?
Is it___? ___?

Then go down the list, muscle-testing or pendling after each question. For instance, you might ask:

Which place is better for making more than enough money to pay my bills? The city.

What is the percent of positivity for this aspect? 90%.

What is the percent of positivity of the country for this aspect? 75%.

You can probe more deeply how to raise the percentages:

Can I raise this percentage for the country? Yes.

By buying a used car instead of a new one? No.

By getting a less expensive house than the one I'm considering? Yes.

How much should I pay per month: $800? $1000? $1200 . . .

Keep a tally of the percent of positivity for each item on your list. You might also ask questions such as: *Which item on this list will be most important to me a year from now? Five years from now?* When you're done, you might find that the country outranks the city seven to four. But you might also decide to go with the city anyway, because the quality of the schools and your higher income ace out everything else. If the process still doesn't clarify the answer, put the question aside and wait a few days. After percolating a while longer in your unconscious mind, the answer may arrive when you least expect it as a sudden, sure knowing.

Along the way, be open to the fact that your very question might be limiting the parameters, and you may want to widen your inquiry by divining your way through more options. For instance, perhaps you can split your time between those two places by pursuing a house share or seasonal rental, or perhaps you would be happier on a beach road than a mountain road. Be creative and receptive to the ideas that flow into your mind, and some surprisingly satisfying options might emerge out of nowhere, so to speak.

"By entertaining multiple factors and perspectives, you're introducing a rich texture into your divining that makes you less likely to override answers with your mind," says Harvey Schwartz. "It can be less immediately gratifying than a one-shot Yes/No answer, but ultimately it is more deeply fulfilling and empowering."

Changing Your Behavior Patterns

By dialoguing with muscle-testing as we go about our day, we can use it almost as a therapeutic tool to meet blocks as they arise and move past them with grace and ease. My friend Kathleen Donovan, a dancer and counselor, is by nature an introvert, and she has blossomed in strength, power, and openness by using muscle-testing for feedback and guidance. She learned it about ten years ago directly from Machaelle Small Wright, and says, "I've developed it so that I can more and more feel the truth of what's deep inside." To help the research for this book, for two weeks she spoke about divining into a tape recorder as she did it.

"When I'm testing, it's the most internal space I can find and so it's a prayerful place," she says. If she needs focus, she'll look at a picture of her late spiritual teacher, Hilda Charlton, yet she doesn't feel the answer is coming from on high. "The more that I come into myself, the more it feels like part of myself as opposed to something separate from me that knows better. It's intimate, like a relationship, not something on a pedestal."

In the two weeks she used muscle-testing, among other things, to decide how many days to go to a healing workshop, whether to buy a certain futon, to select a purse, to reassure herself about a work relationship, to make logistical decisions in a city, to figure out an approach with her landlord, and even to select an e-mail name.

"To me, the process is sacred, but the answer isn't, really," she says. "I hold it loosely. It tells me what's best for me in the moment that I am capable of dealing with, and that might change. It's like being with an enlightened spiritual master. They will challenge you if you're ready, but they won't push you if you're not. And what they tell you isn't always necessarily the objective truth, so to speak—it's what you need to know in the moment."

In those weeks, dialoguing helped her to:

- Stretch beyond her comfort zone. She tested whether to go to a local fund-raising party, something that she would ordinarily find challenging. She got that it would be 90% positive, and she asked why: *Will it help me physically? Emotionally? Mentally? Spiritually? Is it because I'm supposed to meet someone there?* "In the course of asking the questions, something flowers inside me and something new often occurs to me," she says. "Something shifts or opens up. It coaxes me along."

- Manifest a better outcome. Her landlord was balking at returning a rent deposit. "'I used testing to focus my energies on getting it back. I kept on testing until I got a Yes to the question, *Will he return my deposit?* As I was doing it, I was conscious I was making it happen by making myself into the kind of person who would attract that outcome through a combination of firm love, compassion, strength. To get the answer Yes, I had to transmute somehow. If doubt or confusion came in, I kept testing until it got firm again." Another question she often asks is, *Can I do anything to change this?* And then she'll try out ideas that come to mind. "It creates new possibilities," she says.

- Overcome resistance. She was dragging her feet over sending an awkward business-related e-mail to a personal friend she had not seen for some time. She tested to find out what tone to hit and what approach to take. "Testing helped me zero in on my true feelings about the situation, which spurred me on to actually write the e-mail," she says.

- Move away from obsessiveness. On a Sunday, she had an urge to attend a service in the denomination of her youth, and began calling through the phone book to figure out what church to go to. Suddenly, realizing how tense and driven she was feeling, she stopped and tested, *Do I really want to do this?* She got a No. "The testing took me out of my head and into a place where I could quickly perceive my best interest," she says.

"What I really wanted was a deeper experience of Jesus, not a church service."

- Break mental habits. "Testing keeps me from being overly habitual in my thinking—because I'm centering as much as I can, I get new possibilities just automatically," she explains. Raised in a tension-filled family, "I tend to store anxiety in my body and feel exhausted a lot," she says. One afternoon, tempted to call off a demanding task, she asked, *Can I physically do this?* and got a Yes. "Sometimes I get No, but more often, I get that I can," she says. "Testing seems to relax me and stretch my capacity to endure."

- Be honest with herself. She caught herself twice using muscle-testing needlessly. "The truth was, I didn't want to expand in that way. I just wanted to do what I felt like doing." When that happens, she says, she is more likely to be "using it too casually, and it loses its relevance and meaning."

Understanding Obstacles and Unwanted Noes

Sometimes you'll get a go-ahead from divining on a plan or project, but instead of things going speedily and smoothly like you had hoped, obstacles arise in the road like so many speed bumps. Here are some questions that you can ask:

Am I supposed to learn something from this obstacle? Is it on the physical level? Emotional? Mental? Spiritual? Is it about ___? About ____? (Check for different options: it could be about financial management or patience, for example.)

Does this obstacle mean I shouldn't go ahead? Am I supposed to push through it?

Is this obstacle about the decision that I made? Is it about outside circumstances? Do I need to know about these outside circumstances? Is there something I can do about them?

Will _____ approach work for overcoming this obstacle? (Check for different alternatives.) *What is the percent of probability of it working? Percent of possibility? Can I raise those percentages?* (Check alternatives.)

Says Darlene Van de Grift, "Step-by-step, you narrow it down to whatever the pinpoint is, so that you can fix it, heal it, correct it, understand it—whatever you need to do with it to move forward."

On the other hand, sometimes the obstacle seems to be the answer you get with divining! If you keep on asking about something—say, a business opportunity—and you keep getting a No when you dearly want a Yes, here are some questions you might ask:

If I do this anyway, what is the level of stress involved? (Check using percentages or the 1–10 scale.)

If I go ahead, is there a lesson for me to learn from it? (Check such options as money, trust, forgiveness, projection.)

*When I look back on this five years down the line, what
will I see as the percent of positivity about doing it?*

Often, it pays just to put the matter aside at least a few
days to see what happens. Darlene says that when she
can't get a go-ahead through muscle-testing on something she wants, "I'll say, *So you're really telling me that
I shouldn't do this, right? How much percent should I not
do this? Okay. So if I move ahead into the future, is it ever
going to be good for me? Okay, one year? Two? Three?*
Okay, three years down the line it'll be good for me. *How
much negative is it going to be for me between now and
then?* Okay, 100%.

"I'm having a conversation trying to justify what I
want to do, and I go at it in different directions so that
I can get agreement," she says. "But then I finally let it
go. I'll sit with it for two to three days without testing,
and something shifts inside—I don't have to have what I
thought I wanted. Time takes care of it."

CHAPTER 9

ADVANCED TOOLS

EXPLORING OPTIONS FOR ASKING

There are many fruitful ways to converse with the Divine via divining tools. In the following pages, you'll learn how to body-dowse—using your own body as a testing instrument, which involves training it so that your unconscious communicates clearly with you through a particular muscle group. Then you'll find four other options for finger muscle-testing that are more subtle, if you'd rather not broadcast your kinesiology moves; they may also be easier for you to execute. Finally, you'll read brief explanations of three dowsing tools that have unique strengths and can be entertaining to explore.

BODY-DOWSING: WHERE IT COMES TOGETHER

Body-dowsing is where muscle-testing and pendling merge, and it's akin to the type of intuition that reveals itself in body sensations as well.

Body-dowsing involves using the sensations and movements of your body to get a Yes/No answer to a question. Compared to using tools like your fingers or a pendulum, it is more subtle, but once you get the testing pattern established in your mind and body, it can be just as useful.

The trick is to clearly differentiate a particular Yes/No response from the sensations that flood the body when you're excited, afraid, or anxious. For instance, if your No response is a feeling of contraction, it's wise to understand that contraction is also a fear response, and if you avoid ever facing those fears because you think it's divinely spoken, you can lead a stagnant life.

In one form of body-dowsing that's useful when out in public, people ask a question while standing up straight, and then observe whether their body leans forward slightly—Yes—or backward—No. In another variation, people use their arms like weights. They hold them out in front, assign one to Yes and one to No, ask the question, and wait: whichever one drops is the correct answer. Being deeply relaxed—almost in a hypnotic state—helps this to work best. In fact, hypnotherapists call it "ideomotor signaling," and use this approach with clients to bring to light unconscious beliefs and assumptions.

Roberta Godbe, a therapist in San Rafael, California, used this personally when she was trying to decide where to live for a short while between houses. To her left arm she assigned the choice, "Move in with my friend." To her right arm, she assigned, "Wait for something else to come." She found that her left arm barely moved; the right one went down very slowly, so waiting was the right choice. "I like this approach because the unconscious tells me how much weight each option has. Sometimes a hand goes down really fast, which makes it a clear choice, or sometimes they go down together, meaning I could do either one," she says.

Maria van der Schoot of the Netherlands, who teaches intuition courses on four continents, feels a Yes as an enthusiastic sensation throughout her body; No feels like a turning away or distancing. "The way of perceiving is personal to everyone—everyone has their own way of feeling or seeing or hearing answers," she says. "If you feel an answer in a certain way and there's no room for doubt, it's very convincing, then it must be right." If any doubts remain, she suggests asking for a dream that night before you go to sleep or ask for some other sign.

Again, as when you learned the pendulum, you can either ask or train your body. To ask, get into a deeply relaxed state by praying, meditating, or breathing deeply. Then ask your body to give you a clear Yes signal; wait for the response. Once you're received it, ask it to give you a clear No signal; again, wait to receive it. You can also ask for a Neutral response, to indicate that something is not right with the timing or the question.

You can also train your body to speak in certain ways, much like you train your pendling or muscle-testing responses. In a relaxed state, you tell it what you want and nudge it in that direction, doing the calibration questions like those on pages 72–77 until you get a strong, clear response. Here are three such training approaches suggested by Dan Wilson, a British engineer turned dowser:

- Blink. Consciously hold your eyes open and think your question. A blink occurring against your will signifies Yes, two blinks mean No.

- Wrist Twist. Reach out with either hand as though about to shake hands with someone. Ask the question. If your hand twists clockwise, it's Yes; counterclockwise is No.

- Tongue Rub. Run your tongue over the roof of your mouth and ask your question. A rough feeling is Yes, a smooth feeling is No.

You can also body-dowse a map by running your fingers over it with your eyes closed; you'll feel a change in sensation when you're over the target area. I once had a small experience in this. I was looking for a house to buy in Ulster County in the Catskill Mountains, an area in upstate New York with many valleys and hamlets. In my New York City apartment, more out of curiosity and playfulness than anything, I turned over a map of the county so I couldn't see the place names, put it on top of my bed, and with my eyes closed, twirled it around several times so I wouldn't be influenced by knowing what part of the county I was in. Then I ran my right hand over it. I was thinking I might get a buzzy feeling, but what happened is that one spot felt warm. It was so peculiar—I felt around it several times, and it definitely felt a degree or two hotter. I turned the map over to see if anything underneath would cause that. No. The spot was in northwest Saugerties, up by the county line. I went house hunting there and found nothing, but seven months later, a simple, sweet farmhouse came onto the market. I bought it and have lived happily and gratefully there for many years. It was exactly where the warm spot had been, which even to this day I find almost unbelievable, frankly.

SUBTLER WAYS TO MUSCLE-TEST WITH YOUR FINGERS

If you'd rather not have your neighbors staring at you as you move your fingers while testing for the best melon at the supermarket, here are some ways to muscle-test that are more subtle. It's best to first master the basics of testing with the "duck-in-the-hole" technique in chapter 4, but once that's in place and you feel comfortable with the procedures, you might want to experiment with the following to see if you like them better. (Reverse the instructions if you're left-handed.)

With each technique, run though the calibration exercise on pages 72–77, including the sample questions:

Give me a Yes.

Give me a No.

Give me a Choice.

- The Hand Clasp. This is the same as the basic technique, except that you're flipping the left hand over so that it's palm-side down. You're still using your right-hand thumb and forefinger to push against the left-hand little finger and thumb, but because both hands are now palms down, it looks like you're clasping your hands. Your nontesting fingers of the left hand are rest-

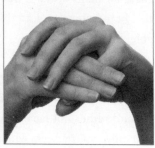

Figure 14:
The hand clasp #1

Figure 15:
The hand clasp #2

ing lightly on your right hand. (Figure 14 is the view looking down; figure 15 is how it looks from the front.)

- Linked Loops. Connect the thumb and pinky finger of your left hand, and insert it into the right-hand first finger from behind; then join your thumb to it from the other side. It will look like the kind of linked chain you see on Christmas trees, with one set of fingers at a 90-degree angle to the other. You test by pulling the right-hand loop to the right rather than by pushing outward. You can also use the left-hand pointer finger and thumb for this.

- Fingers on the Leg. Spread out the fingers of your right hand palm-side down on your right thigh, laying them flat. Tuck the first knuckle of the pointer finger of the left hand in a palm-side-up position under the first knuckle of the right-hand pointer finger. To test, ask the question, press your right finger down while trying to lift the

Figure 16:
Linked loops

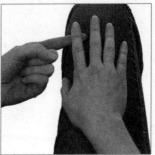

Figure 17:
Fingers on the leg

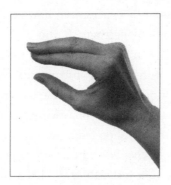

Figure 18:
Middle finger over pointer finger

left-hand finger, using the same amount of pressure in each. If your right-hand finger lifts, the answer is No; if it holds its strength and stays in place, the answer is Yes.

- Middle Finger Over Pointer Finger. Lightly rub the tip of your middle finger over the nail of your pointer finger. If it's a Yes, it should move smoothly; if it's a No, it should feel rougher or stickier. Or press down your pointer finger with the middle finger, taking care to apply equal pressure in each finger. If the point finger holds firm, it's a Yes; if it loses strength, it's a No. (These two techniques are subtle and require precision and focus, but some experienced muscle-testers swear by them.)

TRYING OUT OTHER DOWSING TOOLS

In addition to the pendulum, there are three other major tools used by experienced dowsers, each with its advantages and applications. If you enjoy playing with the pendulum, you'll get a kick out of the gyrations and peculiarities of these other instruments, which you can make yourself or buy online or at a dowsing conference. If you'd like to strengthen your divining skills, you might want to take a workshop from the American Society of Dowsers that teaches you how to use these tools step-by-step. Because your instruction will likely include searching over terrain for verifiable features like water veins and buried objects, you'll get unarguable feedback, and as a consequence, your everyday personal divining will become more precise and, well, grounded!

- Y-rod. This is the most ancient dowsing instrument, the forked stick used by traditional dowsers; today it may be made of plastic rather than willow. Usually one to two feet long, a Y-rod is springy yet strong. It is used most commonly to detect underground water or gas

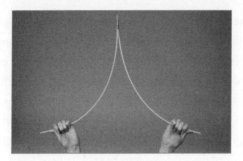

Figure 19: Y-rod

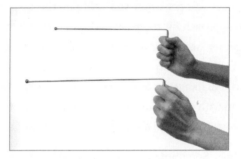

Figure 20: L-rods

veins. You walk over the land holding it with palms up, and it responds with a strong tug downward when you reach the right spot. It can also be calibrated to give Yes and No responses in the neutral or upward positions, allowing experienced dowsers to assess the depth, flow rate, and purity of underground water. To make a Y-rod, cut a two-foot-long forked branch off a tree, or tape two knitting needles together at one end.

- L-rods. These are two rods, from 6- to 24-inches long, with handles at 90-degree angles, which are useful when walking outdoors to precisely locate the outlines of something: a water vein, the best place for a garden or labyrinth, buried objects. The handles are encased in sleeves that allow them to swing freely. Holding one in each hand in parallel position as you would two pistols (but being more relaxed than you would be in a pistol-holding situation!), you ask a question and watch them swing off to each side to indicate a Yes and cross in front to indicate a No (assuming those are the responses you get when you calibrate the L-rods, using the approach on pages 92–94). They can also be used, together or singly, to point out directions—handy if you're lost on a trail somewhere. To make a set, take two coat hangers, cut them with wire cutters, and bend them with pliers into an L shape. Encase the short ends in plastic straws to allow them to move easily.

• Bobber. Sometimes called a wand, this is a 12- to 24-inch springy rod usually weighted at the tip so that it can move in any direction: up, down, sideways, in circles.

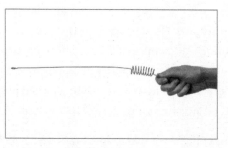

Figure 21: Bobber

Like the L-rods, you calibrate it, and then it can give you a straightforward Yes and No and can also point out directions. It is most often used outdoors to find objects under the ground; its advantage is that it can be used even under windy conditions. It can be purchased, or made by cutting a switch off a tree and taping a coin to the end.

As practical as muscle-testing and pendling are, a third approach—the chits—has unique characteristics that make it useful for those all-too-common times in life when we're emotionally caught up in a decision. In the following pages, you'll learn how this simple process, which has virtually no learning curve, can be applied in turbulent times.

CHAPTER 10

THE CHITS

PAPER-CHASING THE DIVINE WILL

Ronne Marantz, a single mother, was going through a diffi-cult time with her sixteen-year-old son, and the second time he told her to f— off, she had had it. "That is totally unac-ceptable," she said. "If you said that to your football coach, he would kick you off the team—and if you ever say that to me again, you're off the team, because you need parental permis-sion." A few weeks later, he said it again. "My heart dropped into the soles of my feet because I knew I had to do what I had said I would do," she recalls. After he stormed off to his room, she was left in turmoil: football was the most important thing in his life. Can I do this to him? *she anguished.* I don't know if I have the will to follow through. *She couldn't think of any other solution, so in desperation, she wrote out three words on pieces of paper: "Yes"—do it; "No"—don't do it; "Wait"—and see. She folded each one tightly. She prayed with all her might for guidance. Then she threw them down in front of where she was sitting, closed her eyes, moved them around while her eyes were still shut, and reached for one. The answer was* Yes, do it. *So she called the coach the next day and pulled her son off the team. When her son came home from school, he went to his room and cried and cried; feeling that she had Divine backing, she remained firm. "That was the single most important act I did as a parent," she says today. "He never said the word again, he became totally respectful, and today we have a fabulous, fabulous relationship."*

The chits are a little-known but highly useful form of inner guidance. They involve writing out all your options for solving a dilemma on small pieces of paper, and mixing them up. Then you connect deeply with the Divine, throw them, and pick up one—typically the one that lands closest to you or a sacred object. You unfold it and read it. You follow that counsel.

It is a version of the casting of lots, perhaps the most ancient form of divining. In theory, it works like the *I Ching* and the runes, which are also based on random throws of coins, sticks, or stones. Those systems are symbolic—you must interpret the answer through poetic imagery—but the chits give it to you straight, with no wiggle room. That is their strength and gift—and perhaps the reason they haven't spread in use.

Their greatest advantage is that heightened emotion—the kind we flop around in when we're really in a fix—actually makes the chits more, not less, accurate. A highly engaged psyche seems to pull the answer in. This differs from muscle-testing and pendling, where emotions can contaminate the answer, and you may get only what you want to hear. With the chits, you can't even calm yourself by censoring some options. It's important to include answers that you definitely do not prefer, because that opens you up to accepting all the possibilities. That act of surrender raises the stakes, and opens you up to growth and grace.

A DO-IT-YOURSELF *I CHING*

It seems to be a human impulse to invite an answer from the Divine by tossing objects that the Divine can cause to fall into certain patterns, which can then be read for meaning and direction. The casting of lots was practiced in ancient cultures—pyramid-shaped dice were thrown in Ur; sticks of reed, ivory, or wood were used in Egypt; knucklebones from goats and sheep were tossed in Greece and Rome. The Old Testament speaks several times of Urim and Thummim, two stones in the breastplate of the high priests of Israel; some researchers argue that the handful of brief references suggest that they were used when priests were seeking direction, making them most likely a tool for divination.

In 1737, John Wesley, founder of the Methodist Church, was sorely tempted to propose to a woman he had fallen in love with, and he wrote on separate pieces of paper: *Marry, Think of it not this year, Think of it no more.* He chose one at random; it was the last. He wrote in his diary, "Instead of the agony I had reason to expect, I was enabled to say cheerfully, 'Thy will be done.'" He remained single all his life, perhaps helped by the fact that she married someone else almost immediately.

The *I Ching*, based on the random tossing of coins or yarrow stalks, was the major source of inspiration for Confucius and Lao-tsu, whose philosophies of Confucianism and Taoism even today shape character and culture in the Far East. One of the best commentaries on this process was written by Carl Jung in 1949. Asked by Richard Wilhelm to write a foreword to his new translation of the *I Ching*, Jung decided to try the process out for himself. He asked the *I Ching* for feedback on his intention to present its wisdom to the Western mind, threw the coins as the book directs, looked up the hexagrams that resulted, and in response, he writes:

> *The* I Ching *tells me of its religious significance, of the fact that at present it is unknown and misjudged, of its hope of being restored to a place of honor. This seems a perfectly understandable reaction, such as one could expect also from a person in a similar situation.*
>
> *But how has this reaction come about? Because I threw three small coins into the air and let them fall, roll, and come to rest, heads up or tails up as the case might be. This odd fact that a reaction that makes sense arises out of a technique seemingly excluding all sense from the outset, is the great achievement of the* I Ching. *The instance I have just given is not unique; meaningful answers are the rule.*

To him, the *I Ching* was an example of synchronicity in action: it was the coinciding of external events (the throwing of the coins) with an internal event (his question) in a way that was meaningful and that defied cause-and-effect explanation. The *I Ching* was key in Jung's thinking about the concept of synchronicity, and he believed that it and other systems of divination offer a controlled way to tap into that process of meaningful coincidence.

Scientists, of course, have not been believers. Using classic Newtonian science, the uncanny wisdom of the *I Ching* or chits cannot be explained. It's only when we enter the bizarre, inside-out world of quantum physics that some understanding emerges. In a word, it's all connected: our desires, our emotions, the evolving dilemma, the thought to ask the question, the asking of the question, and the falling of folded papers that answers the question—even the solution itself. All these unfold from the unseen order in one piece, so to speak, although we perceive them as happening across time and space. The answer we receive gives our conscious mind the ability to grasp the overall dynamic, attune itself to it, and move forward in concert with it.

The chits are a greatly simplified and precisely personalized version of the *I Ching*. By tossing the chits, we too are summoning answers across time and space that coincide meaningfully with our questions. It can't be explained with the linear conscious mind—"The less one thinks about the theory of the *I Ching*, the more soundly one sleeps," Jung wrote wryly—but on a visceral level, the answers that arrive are zingers that ring true and feel right.

THE INDIAN CONNECTION

I first heard of the chits while visiting South India, where they have been used for at least a century. In 1915 in Kerala, a sadhu—a wandering holy man—gave a spiritually gifted eighteen-year-old the choice of being taught magic, medicine, astrology, the Puranas (scriptures), or Vedanta (nondual philosophy). "I could not make up my mind," the young man wrote years later in *Living with the Master*. "So the sadhu felt that he should leave the decision to God. He wrote the name of each subject on a piece of paper and picked one at random. The slip turned out to be the one with 'Vedanta' written on it." Instruction started that very day, and the youth, who came to be called Kunjuswami, soon became a personal attendant to Bhagavan Sri Ramana Maharshi, a great sage. Ramana, who died in 1951, taught self-inquiry—"Who am I?"—as the means to enlightenment, and although it is a stark and rigorous path, Ramana is also reported to have approved of the casting of lots. In one account in *Arunachala's Ramana*, a devotee cast lots while praying to Ramana and was advised not to carry out what appeared to be a sensible, prudent action. It turned out well, and when he asked Ramana later if that approach was okay for Ramana's followers to use, he wrote, "Bhagavan was pleased to say, 'Yes. It will work if they have faith.'"

In the 1980s, chits were being used in South India at Mata Amritanandamayi's (Ammachi's) ashram in Kerala and at Sri Sathya Sai Baba's ashram in Andhra Pradesh, which is where I first learned of them. "Baba said that if you don't know how to access your higher inner source and you're really uncertain and you want to get some kind of a direction, then use the chits. Trust that it will work for you," recalls Al Drucker, an American lecturer at the college there. "He emphasized that the chits are just temporary props until you come into full self-confidence and learn to trust your own inner source."

For me, the chits quickly proved themselves. I had really longed to travel north, to Ladakh ("Little Tibet"), the last week of my month-long vacation, but had convinced myself it was more "spiritual" to stay at the ashram. The chits said otherwise. In Bangalore, the airline agent very reluctantly sold me the ticket, informing me that I was number 139 on the waiting list for the last leg of my flight, from Srinagar (the plane only held 120). But I trusted, forged ahead, easily got on the plane, and had a magical, even blissful time there. It taught me that spirituality is not the same as dutiful self-sacrifice, a belief I had unconsciously assumed as the oldest of seven children.

Advantages of the Chits
This method of divining has some unique strengths. It is:

- Clear as a bell. The answer cannot easily be misinterpreted.

- Not skewed by our emotions.

- Straightforward to execute, with few steps.

- Somewhat a ritual, which sets a sacred tone for important questions.

- Not a skill that requires practice.

- Easily verified.

Drawbacks of the Chits

This method is:

- Time-consuming and requires a private space.

- Awkward to use in everyday situations.

- Built on trust, which can take time to acquire.

- More directive than participatory.

- Not as easy to dialogue with as muscle-testing or pendling.

LEARNING THE BASIC MECHANICS

Compared to muscle-testing and the pendulum, doing the chits is a breeze, assuming you can write words and tear and fold paper! There are two major variations on the chits:

Multiple Choice

On a clean sheet of paper, starting in the corner, write out all the options you're considering in rows down the left side of the page, leaving white space around each phrase. Alternatively, you can precut pieces of paper in 1" x 1" pieces (or larger, if you like) and write on those.

Let's say, for instance, you've met someone named Chris who makes your heart flutter, but you're getting mixed messages and don't know what to do next. The options might be:

Invite Chris to dinner

Call Chris to ask about a computer problem

Ask Lisa to invite Chris to her party

Let Chris make the next move

Do not pursue Chris. Forget about it!

Now add in these three, which you must always include when doing the chits:

Await another alternative

Do not choose this way (meaning, do not use the chits for this decision)

Tear off each one and fold it up. They can be folded any which way, just so they're more or less indistinguishable from each other. Put them in a small stack, ready for the next step.

Don't limit your options in the hopes of raising the odds of the one you want rising to the top; this is not about odds, but destiny. Often, I've written out more than a dozen options and known deep down which one would land in the #1 position, and it did. I was just loath to accept it initially because it took a lot of courage, money, or faith.

Yes/No Choice

On a clean sheet of paper, starting in the corner, write the following words in a column, leaving white space around each word, or write them on pieces of paper you've precut:

Yes

No

Wait

Wrong question

Do not choose this way

Tear each phrase off and fold it up. Put them in a small stack, ready for the next step.

My friends Gina and Michael use the Yes/No option, and it's kept their marriage going through some rocky phases. Once, after a serious argument, Michael packed up and left. Gina was torn between her anger and her love. She asked the chits, *Should I go get him?* The answer: Yes. She did, and it was a turning point for both. He's also been counseled at key times via the chits to stay with the marriage. Another time, he was giving scant thought to going to an expensive professional conference across the country that he wasn't even sure he had the credentials to apply to. Gina urged him to try the chits, which said Yes, and the event led to sterling contacts, a shift in his research focus, and a job offer.

Choosing the Chit

You have one more decision to make. The #1 chit—the one that shows you the best action to take—can either be the one that falls closest to the sacred object you're using, such as a photo or candle, or the one that falls closest to you. The orientation is up to you; it's whatever feels intuitively right, and it may change over time. If you like, you can figure it out by making two chits—one blank, one with an X—and tossing them with the inner understanding that where the X lands will be the orientation.

POPPING THE QUESTION

The sequence varies from that used for muscle-testing and pendling. One major difference is that you don't have to consciously neutralize your ego and desires. Instead, you're meditating or praying and surrendering internally to the process, which has the same effect.

Step 1. Get Quiet and Connected

The chits are a sacred process: you're communing with the Divine, and that demands a quiet space, inside and out. To do that:

- Find a place and a time of day in which you are sure you won't be interrupted or distracted for half an hour. Sit comfortably, either in a chair or on a pillow on the floor.

- Set up a small altar in front of you. It can be as simple as lighting a candle on the table or floor. If you have an object that represents the Divine to you, you can use that: a symbol or picture or photo, a statue of a deity or saint, a flower, a rock—whatever makes you feel happy and connected to the deepest and truest part of yourself.

- Settle into the silence by breathing deeply, saying a prayer or mantra, visualizing light.

- Mentally dedicate this session to the highest good of all concerned.

Step 2. Write Out the Options

With pencil and paper in hand, write out the chits, either multiple choice or Yes/No. If you're doing the former, make sure that each option is precisely defined and so clear that if it comes up, you have no doubt what it means. It's also very important to include options that you're not crazy about; otherwise, you are limiting the potentiality of the Divine to give you what is truly needed. If you're balking at a particular obvious option, ask yourself, "Am I absolutely sure that this would turn out badly?" and imagine how it might turn out for the best. It's actually when we open to all the alternatives that the chits work most profoundly to move us forward on our path.

Some people prefer to write out the options as the first step rather than the second. Either approach works. But as you write out the options, do it in a quiet, focused state, and you may find new ones popping into your mind. Include them, too. Our receptivity invites these intuitive jumps, which often hit us with an "Uh-oh" and sense of inevitability. Once I had flown from the United States with friends to a breathtakingly beautiful mountain town in India. After five days, one of the men in our party became ill and decided to return to the States. I wrote out chits to

see if I should accompany him to Mumbai, but got a hor-
rifying flash to include the option of accompanying him all
the way back to New York. Sure enough, that was the #1
chit, and I complied under fierce inner protest. His illness
turned out to be altitude sickness, the trip turned out to be
delightful, and it led ultimately to a sweet and significant
relationship. Not only that—six months later, I was offered
a spot on a free media tour of German herbal farms, and
that, combined with frequent flyer mileage credits, got me
back to India free of charge!

Remember also that chits are about actions, not
predictions. If you ask what job to take, that is an action
and you will get the answer you need. If you ask whether
you will be offered a certain job, that's a prediction, and
because the future is in flux and veiled, you can't count
on an accurate reply. In my experience, the chits work
great for action advisories, but fortune-telling is not their
purpose or strength.

Step 3. Pray or Meditate

For at least ten minutes and as long as thirty or more,
focus your energy in prayer or meditation. Ask for the
right answer to be shown to you, as you gently release your
attachment to certain options and accept the possibility
of others. (One way to do this is to imagine how something you want could turn out badly and how something
you don't want could turn out well.) Pray or meditate
until your mind settles down and you feel a deep calm-
ness settle in, and you feel viscerally connected to an

expansive, deep energy. It might feel like a merging of yourself with a higher power, or a going beyond yourself into a sense of pervasive oneness, or settling deep into your innermost self, or an opening wide of your heart, or a sense of deep quiet.

Step 4. Pose the Question

No need to worry about the timing—you'll know when the right moment comes to actually throw the chits: it could be an internal click or shift, or your hands moving on their own accord toward the chits. Pick up the stack of chits, shake them gently between your two hands, and then toss them lightly onto the surface between yourself and the sacred object. Pick up the one closest to you or to the sacred object, depending on your orientation decision. Open it up. That's it!

Sometimes a few will clump together, or two will be almost equidistant from you or the sacred object. Eyeball them and decide which one is #1 before you open them up.

Another option is the one that Ronne Marantz used when in the dilemma about her son. It doesn't require an altar or orientation. Close your eyes, throw the chits on to a flat surface, and with your eyes still closed, reach out and pluck one.

Step 5. Receive the Answer

Check inwardly: on a gut level, does the answer feel right?

The pattern in which the chits fall can be a source of more information, so you might want to open up a few more, especially the chits nearest your choice and the one or two farthest away.

I've found that more often than not, the chits line up in a way that supports the #1 chit: #2 will be conceptually the closest to it, #3 will be also close, and the last chit will be the furthest away from it conceptually. This gives me a reassuring sense of underlying order and harmony.

Other times, the way they fall together can be very helpful in deepening your understanding. A while ago, when I had a soft feeling in the heart for an engaging but emotionally remote man, I got two chits right together in front: *Forget him—he's not the one for you;* and *Use him to further your spiritual growth.* This gave me the understanding to continue to play out that experience not with great hopes, but with the understanding that it was necessary for my learning. The very last one, *Pursue him with ardor,* was also helpful in knowing that was not the best path!

If you get *Do not choose this way* in front, it means you should decide some other way: intuitively, or rationally with research. I sometimes get this when I already know the answer and am simply looking for verification, like when I bought my house in the Catskills. Sometimes when I get *Do not choose this way* as #1, I open up #2 to see what it says, and treat that more as a mild suggestion than a directive. There have been times when I consistently get *Do not choose this way.* When that happens, I back off the chits for some time, because it's clear I'm being nudged into other modes of learning.

On some occasions, as a way of dialoguing, I'll mentally ask for some more information, and will gather up the chits in my hand, close my eyes, and pluck one out. That option, which may or may not be chit #1, is often helpful in answering some other question in my mind.

Because you are opening the door wide with the chits, the counsel you receive can be shocking. The big question, of course, is, do you always do what they say? I do about 95% of the time, because that's how I set up this play of consciousness for myself. I take it seriously, and it takes me seriously, and its guidance has been spot-on for a very long time. To this day, there is only one session out of more than a hundred involving work, spirituality, romance, friendships, and health that makes no sense to me. I was advised to help a friend write a beauty book proposal, which required returning midtrip from India with my boyfriend, writing the proposal, then returning alone to India for a month. The literary agent dropped the ball and the book never sold, to my ultimate relief, since the topic left me lukewarm. Perhaps it was for the highest good of my boyfriend, who, home alone, had bouts of bliss emanating from his Indian experiences and produced some fine paintings, but I don't really know. Yet!

Ultimately, the choice is always yours. If you feel intensely uncomfortable with what comes up, if it doesn't leave you with an "aha" sense of intuitive correctness, or if you just plain don't want to do it, it's your decision and your life! But if you can find the courage in yourself to move forward on something difficult but deep-down right for you, you will be rewarded beyond all measure—guaranteed.

Before you get up and move on, pause and give thanks. You've engaged with the sacred energies of the Divine and received customized guidance; open your heart and affirm your gratitude with words, gestures, a prayer, a commitment.

GETTING SLIGHTLY MORE COMPLICATED

It's possible to devise ways to get a string of answers from the chits, even though they're not as amenable to dialoguing as muscle-testing or pendling. Here are a couple of possibilities:

Dates

If you're trying to decide on a certain date, you can write chits for some possibilities and also make one of the options open-ended: *Shake for the date.* If that comes up as #1, make two sets of chits: one with the months and one with the numbers 1–31. Then you breathe deep, shake first for the month and then for the day.

Two Variables

You can go back and forth between two factors. When I got an inheritance of $32,000 from my father, I made out two sets of chits. One had about a dozen possibilities: *Invest in stock, Buy gold, Put it in savings, Donate it to charity, Loan it to someone in need, Buy a friend's house,* and, as an afterthought, since I was happy living in New York City, *Buy a house in the Woodstock-Saugerties area,* two hours north in the Catskills. The second set of chits consisted of numbers, from $1,000 to $32,000. My thought was that I would get an option from the first set, shake for the amount of money to put into that, then get a second option, shake for the money, and so on, until I had gone up to $32,000. I also put in a chit with just Xs—XXXX—that meant stop! I meditated quite a while, as this was a very big deal, and then got *Buy a house in the Woodstock-Saugerties area*—a big shock to me, but one that filled me with delight. The amount: *$10,000.* And then—*XXXX*. So I stopped. It turned out that $10,000 covered the down payment and closing costs on my Saugerties house, and I spent the other $22,000 on necessary renovations.

GETTING SIMPLER

You can, in fact, use the chits for quick decisions if you can easily access that deep space of connectedness. One technique is to use pre-made chits. If my Indian friend Suno is fixing dinner in her flat and the phone rings with a talkative friend on the other end, she uses a set of Yes/No chits that she keeps by the phone to see if she should pick it up. "Even if you have work to do and it's a chatty friend, there are times it's important to take the call," she says. Another friend who lives in Iran carries paper and pencil with her when she shops and writes out quick chits as needed, shaking them in her hand, closing her eyes, and plucking one. And my friend Tessa, who usually muscle-tests, recently used the chits to decide whether to clean her office, pack for a trip, or join a half-dozen friends at a restaurant where they were getting together with a friend who had moved away. She wrote out the options, prayed for a moment, then threw them in front of her altar. Cleaning her office came up, so without guilt she turned down the dinner invitation. The visiting friend dropped by her place afterward, where they had the kind of quiet, intense talk not possible at a crowded restaurant table.

SIMPLEST YET: COIN-TOSSING

A quick and easy form of the chits is to simply toss coins. This process is so immediate that it's very easy to skip over the quieting and aligning steps, so it's best used for minor matters.

Any coins will do, as long as they're identical, like quarters or nickels. Take two of them and toss them simultaneously. Here's a code:

Heads + heads = Yes

Tails + tails = No

Head + tails = Maybe, Decide some other way, or Wait.

Of course, you could just flip one coin:

Heads = Yes

Tails = No

But having only two options forces the Divine into a black/white choice; a gray zone where some shading is possible improves its usefulness. It's like someone asking if you approve of something they did: you generally want to be able to put some shading into your response.

There's a third method that allows four options for answers. Take two coins that are virtually identical on one side but different on the other, such as the U.S. state-themed quarters. Assign a Yes to the identical side and a No to the nonmatching sides. Then, on the nonmatching sides, make one "higher" and the other "lower" in your mind.

> *Yes + Yes = Yes*
>
> *No + No = No*
>
> *Yes + Higher No = Your choice, but tending toward Yes*
>
> *Yes + Lower No = Your choice, but tending toward No*

Or you can take small, flat stones or buttons and use a Magic Marker or fingernail polish to paint a symbol (such as a heart or an Om) on one side, and a "Yes" and a "No" on the other sides.

> *Yes + symbol = Yes*
>
> *No + symbol = No*
>
> *Symbol + symbol = Wait*
>
> *Yes + No = Wrong question*

You may find that simply tossing the coins in the air gives you the sudden knowledge of what to do. "I'll flip a coin and then when the coin lands—in whichever way it lands—I find out what I really want," says author and teacher Rick Jarow. "The answer is there, and with divination, you just see it—it becomes obvious for the first time." In effect, the process of quieting and focusing your mind clears the way for the answer to come, and the tool may or may not be the way it presents itself.

CHAPTER 11

SUPPLEMENTAL APPROACHES

WAYS TO WIDEN YOUR UNDERSTANDING

We humans are meaning-seeking creatures, say postmodern theorists. It's natural, as we increasingly come into tune with our deeper selves, that we want to know more. Divining lowers our angst over options and eases our way through crises, but as our life becomes both smoother and more adventurous, we often get more curious: What is our path all about? Why this instead of that? Where is it all heading?

We can dialogue using muscle-testing and pendling to ask these kinds of questions. But if you don't find yourself attracted to that method, or if you'd like to explore other ways to widen your understanding, eleven supplemental approaches are listed below. You can dip into any of them as needed, on the rare occasion or on a daily basis—whatever works for you. You can also use them to verify answers you receive from the three tools, especially if major life decisions are at hand. And you may find that one of these approaches becomes your primary guidance system.

These approaches fall into two major categories:

- Direct. These are straightforward ways to communicate one-on-one with the Divine, such as prayers, dreams, and reveries. They require no special tools, just the openness to ask and the willingness to listen.

- Symbolic. These involve using tools—tarot cards, rune stones, *I Ching* coins—that evoke imagery, which in turn is interpreted with the help of a traditional text. Rich in metaphor, these offer a complex picture of a situation's dynamics.

In a sense, it's like the man I once met who was equally fluent in three languages. What language do you think in, I asked him. English, he said, for everyday matters, German when he was trying to solve a difficult problem, and French when he was with his lover. The three major tools covered previously in this book are like major languages, each with its distinctive tone, rhythm, and strengths, and you can mix and mingle them. But it would be a very poor world without Croatian, Bengali, Swahili, and Korean—not to mention Chinese, Japanese, Spanish, and Russian! In the same way, you'll find that each of the following approaches has a distinctive cadence and feel. Some will resonate with you more than others, and all are fun to explore, should you feel the inner urge to do so.

In all cases, be sure to align yourself with the Divine before doing something as simple as pulling a card. This essence-to-essence touching is what engages the deepest and truest part of ourselves and gives the results accuracy and power.

DIRECT APPROACHES: STRAIGHT TO THE SOURCE

It's a receptive, interactive Universe, and when we put out a question, we are guaranteed an answer—if only we are open enough to hear it and willing enough to accept it. The answers can come internally, through a sudden knowing, a strong sensation, words and pictures forming in the mind, or our feet moving in a certain direction. Or they can come externally, through synchronicity and fortuitous events: you may meet a friend with the answer, overhear a conversation, open a magazine to an article, or get an unmistakable sign, such as someone overbidding you on a house you were unsure about buying.

Your desire to know deeper answers will bring the means to you—and it can come in many forms, as Leslie Britt of Seattle learned. She was facing a major decision in her life that was tearing her up emotionally. She prayed for guidance, and pulled a card from a divining tool known as the Cosmic Deck of Initiation. It gave her a clear direction, but she wasn't happy with it. Over dinner that evening, she discussed the issue with her lover, without mentioning the card, and was told the same thing. Angrily, after dinner she went to her therapist, who—again without knowledge of the other advice—told Leslie the same thing virtually verbatim. When Leslie refused to listen, the therapist suggested she draw a rune, and when Leslie did, it was the same message. "I just had to laugh. Like it or not, the guidance was clear," she says. She followed it and realized over time that she had been pointed in the right direction. "It just goes to show how far the Divine will go to guide even a stubborn ass like me," she says.

The following are approaches you can use to get the Divine on the line:

Meditating or Praying

This is the most direct and ancient method of all, used to great effect by billions through the centuries. Its power cannot be overestimated. Praying with all your might for an answer brings the Divine barreling in to respond. It has no choice: that is its job.

Here is one approach. If you have a burning question—the more burning, the better—pray hard or meditate intensely on it for at least half an hour, asking the Divine for an answer in a form you can recognize within the next twenty-four hours. Then let it go. Get up and go about your day. Within twenty-four hours, you'll get direction: it might be an inner voice or picture, a sure knowing, a shift in circumstances, a lightening of the heart, an understanding of a piece of the puzzle, a change in someone else, or a clear sign.

Or you can ask for an answer immediately, as Ronne Marantz did. A prominent educator, she had spent six months pulling together all the pieces for an innovative after-school center that would teach children programs revolving around basic human values such as truth, peace, and nonviolence. She had negotiated with state officials for a license, figured out funding, interviewed teachers, and signed a contract for a property with two buildings. But glitch after glitch arose with the property, and the day she was to sign the final papers, she realized she wasn't 100% clear she should go ahead. So she meditated for half an hour; when she opened her eyes, she knew it was No. Without regret or second thoughts, she dropped her plans for the center. Shortly after, the work of a newly constituted international education committee, to which she had recently been appointed, intensified. This committee was working to establish and consolidate worldwide the same human values curriculum, the Sathya Sai Education in Human Values, which she had been planning to emphasize in her center. The committee required her full attention and necessitated much travel. Canceling her plans left her free to do this work, and ultimately multiplied her overall impact.

Starting Each Day with a Question
In the morning, write your question down in a journal so that it's clear and precise. Then watch what develops in the course of the day to answer it, including synchronicities, songs, overheard conversations, inner shifts, sudden understandings, and phone calls. At night, write down the responses and contemplate what to ask next.

A variation on this is, in the morning, pray for insight and then draw a card from a divination deck such as Angel Cards, the tarot, Archetype Cards, or Medicine Cards, and use it as guidance through the day.

Asking for a Dream
At night, before you go to sleep, write in a dream journal the question that you want information about. Get quiet and connected, in prayer or meditation, and ask the Divine to speak to you through your dreams that night. Keep the journal by your bedside. If you wake up at night with a

dream fresh in your mind, write it down immediately, even if it's a fragment. In the morning, play with it to see what meanings emerge. It's best not to turn to a book that supplies dream interpretations; your unconscious already knows how to speak to you in your own internal language.

With some dreams, the meaning is so immediately obvious that it might make you laugh out loud. Two techniques can help you decode a dream that is more subtle. One is to convert the nouns, or objects, in dreams to words that signify what they represent to you. For instance, if you dream of climbing up a slippery mountain path with a baby bird in your hands that suddenly morphs into an eagle and flies away with you gently clutched in its talons, you could say you have an uphill and risky climb to give life to something grand that then carries you into new territory, whether or not you want to go there—and the entrepreneurial venture you're considering might take on new resonance. Another approach is to go into a meditative or relaxed state and become each object in the dream, one by one, and see what they have to say (the path, the baby bird, the eagle)—since, in truth, each of them is an aspect of your consciousness.

Gwynne Spencer had a dramatic instance of getting detailed information through a dream that she persistently deciphered. When her mother was ill in a hospital, Gwynne dreamed of a little girl in South Africa dressed in a white nylon sheath adorned with ugly red-brown flowers. In the dream were forty-seven people who spoke Afrikaans; they were beating up the little girl, who spoke only English. Gwynne went to her mother's house, lined up all her medications, and opened each bottle. The nineteenth contained red-and-brown capsules. With some trouble, she learned it was an experimental drug that had been tested in a limited trial on forty-seven people in South Africa, where it was made—and it contained lidocaine, a substance her mother was highly allergic to. She checked her mother out of the hospital and put her on an herbal detoxification regimen. Her mother recovered most of her health in two weeks, although the drug had severely affected her eyesight.

Opening Sacred Books

You can seek direction by getting quiet, asking a question, praying for guidance, and then opening up a sacred book, such as the Bible or the Torah or the Bhagavad Gita, at random for an answer. People even use a dictionary for this purpose. (The Grateful Dead got its name when band members opened a dictionary at random; it refers to a song meant to show a lost soul to the other side.)

Sometimes, even without asking, a sacred book can come to your rescue. I was on the New York subway one Halloween, reading *Sri Aurobindo or The Adventure of Consciousness* by Satprem. I had just read a description about how our experience of the outer world changes when we start meditating deeply: "We become extremely sensitive, with an impression of bumping into everything, into gray or aggressive people, heavy objects, brutal events; the world appears enormously absurd." Just at that moment, a man sat down next to me and deliberately bumped into me, hard. I looked up to meet his eyes. Behind the plastic horned Satan mask he was wearing, they were crackling with hostility. I got a shock, but I was so struck by how it matched what I was reading that I found myself chuckling and saying to him in a conspiratorial tone, "You know, you really scared me for a minute!" He gave me a look of disgust and moved on.

Asking for a Sign

All the universe is a sign shop, and you can get your own directional signal by simply asking a question with intensity. "Guidance comes in many forms. It almost never comes from a book or a lecture or something really explicit. It comes from little things," says John Graham, president of the Giraffe Heroes Project, which celebrates people who stick out their necks for the common good. He suggests this exercise: "Assume on your drive home that there's a God-given, cosmic purpose for every time you miss a green light. Instead of tapping your fingernails on the steering wheel impatiently, take that forty-five seconds and look around. Maybe there's a homeless person with a shopping cart and that will mean something to you. Or maybe it'll be a billboard with a message that strikes you, or maybe it'll be the haircut of the guy in the truck in front of you."

Helpful synchronicities can appear in many forms: as singular events, strings of repeating patterns, clusters of recurring themes. What they have in common is that they are outer events that coincide with an inner need, such as an urgent question: they supply information that you need in the moment, if you are open to receive it. You can learn more about how to recognize and increase synchronicity in *The Power of Flow,* the book that my friend Charlene Belitz and I wrote.

Reveries

Hold your question in your mind, and then let it go. Relax so deeply that you're getting a little dreamy. Then watch what images cross your mind. Gently see what information they hold. The art with this is not to censor an image or say, "That can't be it." Work playfully with what comes your way: it's your unconscious trying to reach you in your own language. Scientifically speaking, you're accessing the theta state, associated with sleepiness, lucid dreaming, and hypnosis, when images are freely generated. I had an experience of this years ago without knowing what it was called. I had just finished talking on the phone late at night with my sister Amy, who was feeling stuck and frustrated in her high-pressure job in Indianapolis. As I hung up and drifted off toward sleep, suddenly a vivid picture popped into my mind of Amy walking across a map of Europe with a suitcase in her hand. The next thought was of my frequent flyer miles on Pan Am, some of which were expiring soon. I called and sure enough, I had enough for a round-trip to Europe and I could transfer them to a family member, and so I did. Amy left her job and sold her house in the blink of an eye, then had two magical months hiking in Scotland

and sunbathing in Greece. When she returned, she found a new job in Denver and soon met the dynamic man she would marry. Pan Am collapsed a few months after her trip, so had Amy not used those miles, they would have vanished into the stratosphere!

Writing a Q & A to Yourself

This simple approach is awe-inspiring, because you have visible evidence on paper that you are part and parcel of a wisdom far more profound than your limited concepts of yourself.

It is helpful, when you write your Q & A, to have someone in mind to ask the questions of. It can be God, for instance, or Jesus or Mary or Krishna or an angel or a spiritual teacher or saint or your higher self or your wise self or Universal Consciousness. Neale Donald Walsch wrote his *Conversations with God* series using this method, but it's not limited to a few people with good connections. Anyone can do it.

In a quiet space, at a quiet time of day when you're feeling relaxed, sit down with a notebook and a pen. Align yourself with the Divine by praying or meditating until you feel connected. You might imagine a candle in your heart that fills your body with light and expands to fill the room, the town, the Universe. Then write down a question you're puzzling over. Wait for the answer to enter your mind. "As soon as you write down the question, the answer emerges spontaneously," says intuition teacher Maria van der Schoot of the Netherlands.

"Sometimes even before the question has finished, the answer is already there—and it's often rather short, really spot-on, and concise." Then ask the next question, and the next.

The language may be blunt or sweet, simple or flowery, but you'll recognize it as both a part of yourself and beyond yourself.

This approach has been important to Roberta Godbe on her path. A psychologist and healer, she was in her early twenties when she read instructions in a book named *The Impersonal Life* on how to dialogue with the Divine. It read in part:

Ask me a question. Then, with a silent, earnest prayer to Me for an answer, but without anxiety, care or personal interest, and with an open mind, wait confidently for the impressions that will come.

Should a thought come that you recognize as what you have read or heard somewhere, cast it out immediately and say, "No, Father, what do You say?"

Other thoughts may come from other human sources, but if you are alert you will recognize them as such and refuse to accept them. Then, if you persist in asking Me, you will finally get an answer that you will feel is from Me.

Thus it will be at first. When you have learned to distinguish My Voice from all other voices, and

*can keep your personal interest wholly suppressed,
then will you be able to hold silent communion
with Me at will, without interference from others'
ideas, beliefs, and opinions; and you can ask any
question you wish . . . , and I will that moment
place in your mind the words to speak.*

When she first did it, she recalls, "All of a sudden a flow
of guidance came through that would speak through me.
Then my mind would go: 'You're making this up. This
is ridiculous.' Then the sweet flow would keep coming
through. Even though my mind was going quack, quack,
quack, it would still keep flowing. When I wrote it down,
I'd read it and think, 'This is not how I talk or think or
speak,' so it further validated things." When she needs
guidance on major matters like her relationship and
her house near Mount Shasta in northern California,
she often goes to a favorite spot on the mountain, where
she sits and relaxes as she asks for inner guidance.
She usually follows the reflections or guidance, but
one time balked at selling her beautiful house; when
she didn't, her health became compromised from
environmental toxins.

I used this Q & A approach to get more information
about writing this book. Some of it went like so:

Q: Why are you asking me to write this book?

A: It is what you want.

Q: In what way?

A: *On a soul level, it is something you must do.*

Q: *Isn't divining less evolved than intuition?*

A: *Not less evolved, just different. They teach different lessons.*

Q: *Does one inevitably move past divining?*

A: *One inevitably moves past everything on the journey to the Self.*

Q: *Who is giving me the answers?*

A: *The same One who is asking the question.*

Q: *So it is a dialogue with myself? Why?*

A: *For your own amusement.*

Q: *If I suddenly stopped, would the same answers come to me?*

A: *No, because then you would be on a different learning path.*

Q: *A better one?*

A: *Only if the time is right and the need is there.*

This could easily, of course, be a play of my own mind, but having it down in words has been very useful. And since everything is a play of mind, why not have fun with it?

SYMBOLIC APPROACHES: A PICTURE IS WORTH A LOT

Like the chits, symbolic systems are based on randomness from which wisdom inexplicably emerges. Unlike the chits, they speak in a rich metaphorical language that you decipher and apply to your situation. Often the meaning is unmistakable; other times, you'll have to work with it to understand it. Each system has a distinct sensibility, its own vocabulary, and enough intricacies that hundreds, if not thousands, of books are written about them. Because of their complexity, they are beyond the scope of this book, but you'll find in appendix 2 some suggested sources for exploration.

Their great strength is that they can give you an overview of a situation. It is like looking down upon a crossroads from high above, so you can see the terrain, where different roads lead, and encounters and obstacles that might occur on the way. Their drawback, however, is that your own desires and blocks can color your interpretation, the learning curve can be daunting, and you don't always get straightforward or comprehensible answers. Still, they can deepen your intuition and be fun to explore, especially if you are metaphorically inclined.

You don't have to neutralize your hopes and emotions with these systems; in fact, the more aroused your psyche, the more pointed the reading is. Still, make sure you are in a quiet, connected, and receptive state when you pose the question and look up the answer in the text.

I CHING

This venerable 5,000-year-old system has the sensibility of a wise, strict, and kindly elderly uncle; it hits home with stunning accuracy. Incorporating both Confucian and Taoist thought, the *I Ching* is concerned not just with an answer to a specific question, but with understanding the larger dynamics unfolding in the matter at hand. Jung called it "one of the oldest known methods for grasping a situation as a whole and thus placing the details against a cosmic background." With imagery that invokes mountains, thunder, and streams, it counsels patience, modesty, forbearance, courage, the inevitability of change, and moving when the timing is right.

Also known as the *Book of Changes,* its interpretations are based on sixty-four hexagrams. These were once derived from tossing turtle shells in a fire, but these days they are derived from tossing three coins six times. You write down the pattern they fall in, and consult the book to find out its significance. If all three coins land on the same side, that's a changing line, and the hexagram morphs into a second one, which can show you the direction of a dynamic. The most esteemed version in the West is Richard Wilhelm's; later versions offer more modern language.

The Tarot and Other Card Systems

If the *I Ching* is an uncle, the tarot feels like a chatty, wise, and mysteriously eccentric elderly aunt. Its origins are arcane and debated: its imagery has elements that harken to the Kabbalah, the Jewish mystical tradition, as well as to Egyptian, Greek, and Indian mythology. Early references to it are found in fourteenth-century French reports, and some believe that it originated in India and was carried to Europe by the Romany, or gypsies.

Just as a deck of playing cards has face cards and number cards in four suits, a tarot deck has a Major Arcana of twenty-two cards and a four-suit Minor Arcana of fifty-six cards. There are literally hundreds of tarot deck designs, many of them created in the last few decades with a playful hand, including an angel tarot, teddy bear tarot, and cat tarot. But the classic deck that most others play off of is the Rider-Waite-Smith deck, which features symbols such as cups, swords, staffs, and coins.

When you do a tarot reading, you lay the cards out in certain spreads; each card's position determines the significance of that factor in the overall picture. Taken as a whole, the spread can reveal the underlying energies of a situation and show you ways to move effectively through it. Tarot can be interpreted strictly by the book, by looking up each card's assigned meanings, or it can be used as a springboard to insight by seeing what stories emerge in your mind from the pictures. Because of their rich imagery, they lend themselves to imagination and creative interpretations. They can also be used more simply. One friend, who often ribs me about muscle-testing, let slip that he draws three cards in the morning to get a sense of what the day might bring.

A number of other card systems are more recent in origin and simple to use: you merely ask a question, draw a card, and read the result, often printed on the card itself. These too can be arranged in spreads. Perhaps the most popular of these are the Medicine Cards, which are illustrated with forty-four animals that have been used by

Native Americans as teachers and guides. The Archetype Cards, by spiritual teacher Carolyn Myss, help you to delve deeply into your underlying psychological patterns. Angel Cards, which invoke a singular quality like Patience or Spontaneity or Surrender, can also work for divining, as my friend Lakshmi discovered. She calls herself a "hard-boiled egg" but harbors a tenderness for angels, and one night at 1 a.m., restless over whether to attend a ten-day silent Vipassana meditation retreat, she got out of bed and pulled an angel card: it was Retreat. It shocked her into following through, although it wasn't the timing or location she had anticipated. Afterward she said, "It was exactly, exactly what I needed. It totally cleared away the emotional residue of a very hard year."

The Runes

The earliest runic symbols, carved onto rocks in Sweden, date back more than 2,300 years to the Bronze Age. The symbols were absorbed into evolving alphabets, but they also had an alternate path, as divining tools and magical talismans. Many of the original divinatory meanings have been lost through the years, particularly because of religious persecution in the seventeenth century, but they've enjoyed a worldwide revival in the last forty years, based on reinterpretations of the ancient symbols. Runes today are usually ceramic or wooden; you can easily make your own or purchase them in a bookstore or over the web.

Like the *I Ching*, the runes put your decision into a larger context. To cast the runes, you ask a question, pull a rune out of the bag or toss them, and read the interpretation. You can also lay out simple spreads to gain a more complex understanding of a situation; for example, a three-rune spread could point to the past, present, and future. For the explanatory text, you can use a research-based approach like that of Edred Thorsson or an intuitive-based approach like that of Ralph Blum.

EXERCISE
STEPPING OUTSIDE A MOLD

This exercise is a tribute to Hilda Charlton, my first meditation teacher, who would playfully and wisely counsel her students, "Break a mold, kids!"

First, try out one of these supplementary approaches that intuitively appeals to you. What did you learn about yourself? Now, with an open mind, try out an approach that doesn't appeal to you at all, perhaps one you select by divining. What did you learn about yourself?

In the preceding pages, you've learned of tools and approaches that can help guide you through the challenges of your life. The more you use them, the more skillful you'll become at navigating rocky shoals and the smoother your passage through rough waters will become. Yet there may come a time when you find the questions themselves disappearing, along with your need to know answers.

EPILOGUE

CAN WE GO BEYOND CHOICE?

When I was trying to figure out how to write this book, I was stumped about how to organize it. I knew all the pieces, but couldn't figure out a structure that made sense. Reading over my old diaries, I came across an account of a reverie—a technique I hadn't used for some time—so I tried that. And the image that popped up was . . . Frosty the Snowman! And this was in the heat of India, so it wasn't inspired by the weather. I tried to push the picture away, but quickly got smart and examined it. Suddenly, I got the structure. The "old silk hat" was the mystery and magic of divining; the head was cognitive information, such as its history and science; the midbody with arms the basic how-to; and the base the tools themselves. Frosty himself was playful—he was dancing around—and although considered a fairy tale by some, the children knew him to be real. At the end, he melted away—we could say, merged into his essence. (A year later, when I was writing the book in South India, in a shop I saw a card that had a banyan leaf with a hand painting of Frosty—not a common image there. And he was leaning toward a smaller snowman whom he had his arm around, as if giving information!)

So now we are at the melting-away part of the book.

You will find that as time goes on, divining moves from being outside you to inside you, and soon to an even deeper place within. Then the questions start melting away; you know the answers almost before you ask. At some point, the answers themselves become less important. Like Diane Bull, you find that your feet take you where you need to go. You are aligned with your Essence, and you find that you are always where you need to be.

Indians speak of two major spiritual paths: devotion, called *bhakti,* and knowledge, *jnana.* The devotional path is one of love and surrender, of merging with Divinity through the form that most draws you. It is a sweet and tender path, full of a feeling of protection and guidance. In many ways, divining is a devotional act: by doing it, you devote yourself to the highest good, to God, and you are taken care of.

The path of knowledge is a more severe one: it demands deep knowledge of the self, of who you are at the deepest, truest level. The basic question used in meditation is "Who am I?" There is no answer, just a burrowing deep into a sense of a vast, love-saturated emptiness. On this path, which naturally follows *bhakti,* ideas of cause and effect, true and false, right and wrong, melt away; they are seen as mental concepts that cloud the experience of ultimate reality.

As we move along our spiritual path, we may find that we use divining less. This has been happening to me, bit by bit. It is disconcerting but the timing is right, and I can see where, in a subtle way, I had become attached to knowing answers as a form of security. Now, I am more often hanging out in the "I don't know" zone, and my task is to become comfortable with that utter lack of a framework in which to think and act.

This is the paradox: through divining, the need to know evolves into "I don't need to know," and that is where the ultimate mystery lies.

It's from that perspective that questions about divining are most compelling to me now:

Q: Who exactly is giving the answer?
A: The same One who is asking the question.

My understanding is that this underlying force, this Essence, is the one asking the question as well as giving the answer. And, in fact, the answer may be there before the question: it may be a movement in the universe seeking expression, guidance seeking a form in which to be heard. We are the instruments through which this asking and answering move. Through our minds, hearts, and bodies, the Divine experiences the trials, doubts, and delights of life.

At some point, we realize that from the deepest perspective it doesn't matter what we do—all is God, all is good. "Henceforth I ask not good fortune—I myself am good fortune," is how Walt Whitman put it. When this occurs, trust has nothing to do with trusting it will turn out all right. It is simply moving in flow with the moment without critiquing or second-guessing the stream of events coming our way—living spontaneously.

This doesn't usually happen overnight. Often we have to practice trust a long time first, and divining is one of the best ways to build that skill.

Until then, as Byron Katie wisely counsels, "Don't pretend yourself beyond your evolution." Muscle-testing, pendling, and the chits propel us beyond our limited minds into the wisdom of the Universe, in the most helpful and practical of ways. As one Indian guru put it: "We don't need astrology, but if it's going to rain, we might as well have an umbrella!"

TROUBLESHOOTING GUIDE

WHAT TO DO IF A TOOL FALTERS

Can divining go wrong?

The good news is that from the highest perspective and in the truest sense, the answer is no. Divining cannot go wrong. Everything is the Absolute, God, Essence, Source, Unified Consciousness, and all that unfolds is Divine Will, even so-called mistakes and misdirections. So when divining doesn't seem to work, that too is all in the plan. "What is, is God," says spiritual teacher Byron Katie. "How do I know that? It rules—absolutely."

But part of that Divine Plan may be for us to learn from divining as we go along. The clearer we are inside, the clearer our divining will be—and in fact, divining can be a tool that helps us achieve greater clarity in life. When divining doesn't seem to make sense, that too is useful information. What blocks us in divining may well be what blocks us in life, so in figuring out why and what it means, we learn much about our motives, projections, and path. It drives us deeper, and that ultimately makes our divining—and our lives—truer.

There's a definite learning curve to divining, with ups and downs as part of the process. "At first there's a beginner's lag, when your dowsing muscle doesn't have enough strength, and disappointment can put mental blocks in your mind," says master dowser Bruce Irwin. "But the more you tune that dowsing muscle, the stronger it gets. Everything is inside you." So inaccurate readings, too, are a gift, as is everything else that throws us for a loop. "Everything happens *for* you, not *to* you," says Katie—a wise mantra for life in general.

Speaking relatively then, divining can go offtrack in three ways:

1. Problems with the practical how-tos.

   Divining is not a loosey-goosey affair. To get useful information, we need to be clear, focused, and balanced, and at times it's quite natural for us to go awry, especially when we're first learning. Read through the Divining Checklist and the section that follows to pinpoint the cause if your answers become puzzling, inaccurate, or don't play out over time.

2. Pitfalls in how we apply divining to our lives.

   Some seductive ways of thinking and acting about divining may ultimately sabotage us and lead us down some strange roads. Some of these pitfalls are blatant, some subtle. In the second section that follows, you'll find out what these are and how to sidestep them.

3. Doubts coming from yourself or others.

   Since learning to divine is fundamentally learning to trust ourselves, self-doubt can hobble our efforts, so you'll also find information on what kinds of doubt can arise and how they can be addressed. And you'll

find suggestions on how to deal with friends and
family who are skeptical of your new approach.

I've offered a few solutions in the Divining Checklist,
but remember that divining is a creative process, and
as you go along, you may find solutions of your own
that work better, as well as problems and pitfalls not
covered here. Trust your own findings and move with
them. Your own consciousness is crafting your process
and must be honored.

Also, remember that motivation matters. Putting
your heart into divining and doing it sincerely is far more
important than getting every detail right. We are granted
a huge leeway for mistakes. I personally have made all the
errors listed and yet have still been pointed in the right
direction; it just took a little longer or went a more circu-
itous route. In fact, while writing this book, the Universe
kindly gave me a minicourse in how not to divine: everything that could go wrong, did, and in the process of figuring out why, I developed a much keener understanding of
the ins and outs of divining. We get what we need—but
only always!

DIVINING CHECKLIST

If you are running into a snag with a tool, look through this list—or divine your way through it— to find some helpful solutions.

Physical

___Are you exhausted?

See page 251.

___Are you ill or on strong medications?

See page 257.

___Are you feeling spacey or disconnected?

See page 256.

___Are you dehydrated?

See page 256.

___Are you having an "off day"?

See page 259.

___Are your surroundings hectic?

See page 104.

Emotional

___Are your emotions in overdrive?

See page 255.

___Do you badly want a certain outcome?
See page 253.

___Are you trying too hard to get it to work?
See page 76.

___Are you ambivalent about hearing the answer?
See page 254.

___Are you overusing it?
See page 255.

___Are you divining from greed, not need?
See page 258.

___Are you engaging in wishful divining?
See page 252.

Mental

___Is the question unclear?
See page 250.

___Did you lose your focus during the questioning?
See page 124.

___Are you skipping the step of asking permission?
See page 122.

___Do you not really need the information?
See page 250.

___Are you feeling impatient or rushed?
See page 254.

___Do you have an opinion that you're trying to get backing for?
See page 256.

___Are you full of doubts about the tool?
See page 268.

___Are you doing it too casually?
See page 258.

___Are you rechecking too often?
See page 136.

___Are you trying to force some process with your will?
See page 253.

___Are you holding the answers too tightly or rigidly?
See page 260.

Spiritual

___Are you skipping the step of making a deep inner connection?
See page 107.

___Are you moving ahead without that gut-level Yes?
See page 128.

___Are you asking about the future?
See page 253.

___Are you always overruling the guidance?
See page 255.

___Are you feeling special because you're good at divining?
See page 257.

___Are you rushing some process that needs time to unfold naturally?
See page 264.

___Are you overdoing divining?
See page 258.

___Are you being nudged into other decision-making modes?
See page 259.

X-factor

___Are you using it for medical diagnosis?
See page 265.

___Are you getting into someone else's business?
See page 265.

___Is it possible you aren't supposed to know the answer yet?
See page 267.

___Are you supposed to use some other means of deciding?
See page 264.

PROBLEMS WITH THE PRACTICAL HOW-TOS

Below is a list of practical problems that can cause divining to go awry. To track your patterns, keep a written record of what you divined for and what the answers were. This will help you figure out which of the following factors might be causing static in the wires.

Asking Foggy Questions

Questions must be crisp, clear, and to the point. The words must be concrete, specific, and free of double meanings.

Some solutions: Write your questions out and edit them down so they're crystal clear and easily answered with Yes or No. Read them out loud to see how lucid they sound. If your questions tend to wander on, work with a clearheaded friend to pare a complicated issue down to a set of basic questions. You can also set a word limit of ten or fifteen, say. Or, for fun, play Twenty Questions with a friend to hone your skills. In this game, one person thinks of an object like a book, place, or person, and the other person can ask up to twenty questions to zero in on it—but the answer can only be a Yes or No.

Asking When You Don't Really Need the Information

If you're asking a question out of idle curiosity, you might get metaphorically slapped via a blatantly wrong answer. It also seems that the more your divining evolves, the less information you're allowed—perhaps to keep you in the moment and not the future. A friend of mine from

Prague was arriving on the train at some unknown point in the Indian town I was staying in, and although it didn't matter to my schedule, I was curious if he had arrived or had been delayed. I got 100% wrong answers—and it hadn't even been necessary to ask, because when he knocked at the door that evening, I had finished my work and was available.

A solution: Ask not out of curiosity but out of need. Play a game with yourself: instead of trying to suss something out far in advance, see how close in time you can get to an event before you divine for direction.

Being Misaligned: Uncentered, Nervous, Exhausted

If you're having an important conversation with someone you love, being centered, calm, and fully present will give you the best outcome. Divining works the same way. When we're discombobulated or overtired, our circuits are overloaded and distortions can easily occur. We may, in fact, get exactly the opposite answers if we're severely conflicted or thrown off balance in some way, something dowsers refer to as "polarity reversal."

A solution: If you're not in the best shape, postpone your divining for a few hours or days, and treat yourself gently and lovingly in the meantime. If you need an answer sooner rather than later, use blind-testing, preferably with a calm, unflappable friend. And double-check your polarity by asking the question, *Is my name [your name]?* If you get a No, adjust your polarity using an acupressure technique: with the side of one hand, tap the side of the other hand ten times on the area between your little finger and wrist.

Wanting Agreement, Not the Truth

If you want the truth of a matter, divining will respond with alacrity. "It's like a friend with a velvet scalpel: it's going to gently cut right through to the truth," says dowsing teacher Marty Cain. But if you'd rather have agreement or reinforcement, be careful—that desire can influence the answers you get. You'll be reassured, but still, alas, clueless.

Some solutions: Ask yourself deep down: "What do I want most?" It's like raising a child: would you rather he or she tell you what's really happening in their life, or parrot what you want to hear? Set your intention when you start your session with a phrase such as, *Please give me the truth and the truth only*.

Not Wanting Divining to Work

A friend told me, very happily, that she had carefully followed pendling instructions and it hadn't worked for her. Small wonder: her passionate belief in following her heart's guidance is what steers her beautifully through her days.

A solution: Divining is not needed here! It amplifies intuition, and if your intuition is already at high volume, no problem—although it might be useful as an occasional backup for those times when overwhelming emotions render intuition mute.

Asking About the Future

It is human nature to stray in this direction, but the answers you get to questions like, *Will ____ happen to me? Will I get that particular job/house/opportunity? Will ____ ever fall in love with me?* tend to be a frustrating mixture of right and wrong, or just flat-out wrong.

Some solutions: Only ask questions about the future when you need to make practical arrangements for things like child care and airplane tickets. If you can't stop yourself from peering ahead, ask, *What is the possibility of this happening? The probability of this happening?* and check for the percentages—realizing that this figure can change from one moment to the next, and itself has a high probability of error. Then use that figure to brainstorm ways to improve the odds (see page 153).

Being Willful or Having a Strong Opinion

Divining is a delicate dance of opposites: we must be relaxed yet alert, receptive yet enterprising, engaged yet neutral. If you have a strong will that you impose on the divining process, you will override this balance and merely get the answers you want—not that useful in the end. If you are divining to get more backing for a strong opinion you already hold, you'll probably get a Yes—and the Divine will have to get its real answer out to you through the unfolding of events that may turn your opinion upside down.

Some solutions: Try out, one by one, the neutralizing strategies on pages 110–115, until you find one that fits your mental and emotional style. Or if the prayer "Thy will be done" resonates with you, say it before you divine, and don't start until something shifts internally and you really mean it.

Being in a Purely Mental Space

Divining is a full-spectrum experience that unites the head, heart, and body. The head figures out the question and interprets the answer; the heart connects us to the Divine; the body performs the actions and gives us intuitive signals. If you are totally in the mind, divining can quickly become dry, mechanical, and shallow. One clue: you'll become impatient while doing it.

Some solutions: Before you divine, slow down, take a deep breath, and check out your physical and emotional sensations. What are you feeling in your body? Your emotions? Stay with it until they click in, and then proceed. Or take yourself through the meditation on page 115.

Not Wanting to Know the Answer

Sometimes in our gut we know exactly what we have to do but we just don't want to do it, so we may unconsciously use divining to throw up a confusing smoke screen that gives us contradictory or fuzzy advice. Anything to stall it off!

A solution: Self-honesty is the only way out of this dynamic. Think of your biggest fear about moving forward and ask yourself, "Do I absolutely know that this is true? Who would I be without this thought?" If the action involves you leaving a situation, remember: if you don't leave a situation when the timing is right, it leaves you. The things you're sentimental about are wont to change in ways you won't like.

Always Overruling It

You can set it up as you like, but if you're only asking for a second opinion and you're not even listening, then you'll find divining getting balky. Wouldn't you react the same way to being ignored?

A solution: Run an experiment. The next three times you divine, carefully follow the guidance. What happens?

Being Emotionally in Overdrive

Sometimes, hard as we try, we can't stop the emotions surging through our mind and body, especially on long-standing triggers. When we're in the midst of experiencing what Eckhart Tolle calls the "pain-body," it's running the show, and it may take all our effort simply to notice that fact.

A solution: Forgo muscle-testing or pendling for the moment. Breathe deeply and take a run, a walk, a nap, to let your emotions abate—they inevitably run their course if you aren't encouraging or fighting them. Then see if you're calm enough to divine. If you do need an answer immediately, blind-test to remove emotional contamination or use the chits, making sure to calm and center yourself during even that process.

Being Dehydrated

A lack of water can hamper the flow of energy through your electrical system, which can throw off the results of pendling and muscle-testing.

A solution: Drink!

Not Being Grounded

Strong energies can run through our bodies when we divine. If you find yourself getting too spacey, take a short break. Then . . .

Some solutions: Plant your feet on the ground and imagine roots growing out of them deep into the center of the earth. Or raise your arms above your head, hold them there a moment, then lower them straight to the sides with an audible "Whoosh!" Or zip yourself up, as though you're zipping up a jacket, by running a hand from your pelvis to your lips (about three inches out from your body) three times. Or try this strategy: say, "Chocolate cake" over and over until you can almost taste it.

Opinion-Seeking

Our divining is our unique play of consciousness, and when we go beyond honest, actionable questions into seeking verification in the realm of opinion—*Which political party is best? Which newscaster is the most honest?*—we are getting a personalized answer that mirrors our own mental patterns and needs, rather than, shall we say, the Absolute truth. We all have our roles to play that divining ushers us toward—which may involve being an ardent Democrat or devoted Republican—but that doesn't make it the Word from Beyond for anyone but yourself.

A solution: If you feel you're divining so that you can out-argue someone, back off. A clue: you can't wait to confront a particular person with your answer. Respect divining's sacred energies, and save it for those times when you really need an answer to move forward in your life.

Illness, Fatigue, and Medications

If you are in pain or have little energy, you may not be able to marshal the clarity of mind to ask a question via muscle-testing or pendling and take in the answer. Some medications, too, may make you drowsy or impede your thinking.

Some solutions: Wait for a time, or a time of day, when you're feeling as good as possible. Or use a simple system like the chits. Or work with a trusted divining friend who can do the actual testing or pendling for your questions.

Being Demanding

If you're getting fuzzy answers that change quickly, it could be because you're using your will to stampede the process. Sometimes I have found myself insisting on having an answer right this moment, as a way to control uncertainty, anxiety, or mental restlessness. It's a demand of the Universe, rather than an easing into the flow of it, and—just like a human who is prodded—the Universe gets balky.

A solution: Ask straight out, *Is this the right time to ask this question?* Or, *Do I need to divine about this?*

Grasping

In theory, divining should work for ventures like winning the lottery and horse races: isn't the abundance of the Universe limitless? In practice, no one seems to be able to make it work for gambling or ill-gotten gains very well or for very long.

Some solutions: "Dowse for need, not for greed," say dowsers. Get a sense of what greed feels like on a visceral level—it might be as primal as salivating—and be alert for the times it arises so that you can back off divining, in order to keep yourself out of trouble. Perhaps the best antidote for greed is gratitude, which you can easily foster by keeping a nightly or weekly list of small and big things you're thankful for.

Divining Too Often or Too Casually

There's no rule on how often it's good to divine—it's what works for you in the moment—and especially in the beginning, as we're learning, it's fun to try it out in lots of ways. But if you're starting to get a feeling you're using it too casually and, yes, too obsessively, it may be wise to step back from it for a while.

Some solutions: Take a break for a day, a week, even a month. Or limit it to certain kinds of decisions. And if you find yourself frenetically pendling or testing through, say, a daily to-do list, try this: Sit still. Do nothing. No books, no music, no TV. Nothing. Just sit. Your questing and questioning mind might get noisy, but if you don't feed it with questions and answers, it will calm down. Says Carolyn Touryniere, "You'll be surprised—if you sit down, lots of things will come to you intuitively. And half those things on your list that you were going to ask about, you realize they don't have to be done today, or tomorrow, or at all."

The Winding Down of That Approach for You

Divining may be simply a stage of learning for you, and the sign that it is drawing to a close is that the answers you get, no matter what system you use, will stop making sense, and this will go on for an extended period of time.

A solution: Back off divining for a while. Try it again in a few weeks or months, and if it still doesn't work, give thanks for what you've learned and move on.

You're Having a Bad Day

Maybe it's biorhythms or crossed stars or an underlying bad mood, but some days divining simply doesn't work as well as on other days, just like some days you won't write or paint or play racquetball as adroitly.

A solution: Lay off divining and do something laid-back, like listening to music, digging into a novel, or strolling through nature.

WHEN WHAT SEEMS WRONG, ISN'T

Sometimes answers that we peg as wrong are simply misinterpretations or misunderstandings of the ways in which the Universe flows and divining works. For example, an answer may seem wrong on the surface but may actually be right for you if:

You've Not Grasped the Whole Picture Yet

Maybe the answer is right but your comprehension is imperfect. Sometimes—in fact, often—our knowledge comes in fits and spurts of insight. For example, a friend lies about something minor that makes little sense at the time; only later, after similar things occur, do we see how it revealed a larger truth about his character. In the same way, an answer may not compute at first. Later, as events unfold, it may make total sense.

A solution: Don't toss a strange answer into the wastebasket. Put it on a shelf in the back of your mind and check later to see if it revealed something important. Writing it down in a notebook might be useful for later.

It's a Stepping-Stone Instead of a Final Step

We can't always get there from here. Sometimes we can only see so far, and our divining will deliver us to that point so that the next step can present itself. This is where we learn to pivot on a dime and move in accord with the moment.

A solution: Don't be rigid or orthodox about a particular answer being the final one. Stay alert for signs or synchronicities that point you in another, even wildly different, direction.

It's Pushing You into a Larger Process

Sometimes we need to get smart about something, and a Yes or No is simply the kick that propels us into the thick of the lesson. When I was in Lumbini, a dusty Nepali village where the Buddha was born, I tested to see if I should move from a slightly run-down travelers' lodge to another that the guidebook described as more upscale, and got a Yes. I went to look at it, and every other lodge in town, and came back with fresh appreciation for mine, by far the best. I tested again and asked, *Does it matter where I stay?* No. Although the Yes seemed wrong, it put me into a process that ended my mental restlessness and allowed me to settle back in with gratitude.

A solution: Treat an answer like a clue in a treasure hunt and follow it to see where it leads you.

The Universe Has Something Else in Mind

What seems like a wrong answer may be the Universe directing things behind the scenes to stop you from going in the wrong direction. As Leroy Bull puts it, "It gets apparent over time that the answers you get are almost always either correct, or it's what the Universe wants."

A solution: Play with the idea, what if your "wrong" answer is actually correct? How might that play out over time? Let your imagination play with the range of possibilities. For inspiration, recall the story of the Chinese farmer (a tale no good spiritual book can go without!). When his field horse escaped into the hills, his neighbors sympathized with him, but he replied, "Bad luck? Good luck? Who knows?" A week later, the horse returned with a herd of wild horses, and when his neighbors congratulated him, he replied, "Good luck? Bad luck? Who knows?" Then his son, trying to tame one of them, fell off it and broke his leg. "Bad luck? Good luck? Who knows?" said the farmer. Some weeks later, the army marched into the village and conscripted every able-bodied youth, but let the boy go because of his broken leg. Now was that good luck? Bad luck? Who knows?

WHAT TO DO WHEN YOU GET A WRONG ANSWER: PLAYING SHERLOCK HOLMES

Wrong answers, in themselves, can be like clues in a mystery book. If you examine them closely and decode them, you'll be guided into new understandings that can ultimately turn out to be even more useful than right answers.

Lately I have found that when I am idly curious about something, divining won't cooperate. It used to and it was a lot of fun, but now I'm being taught different things, it seems.

This became clear when a friend and I were stuck in an airport deep in the Himalayas in Nepal after a trek. For the second day, there was a strong chance that all flights in and out would be canceled due to bad weather. I muscle-tested on the probability of us making it out by plane that day: 100% probability. Great! A half hour later, they announced the planes were definitely *not* flying. Bummer! We ended up piling into a weather-beaten four-wheel drive full of boisterous Italian trekkers and traveling overland by jeep, foot, and rickety bus. We arrived at our destination twelve hours later, at midnight—too late to get into my small hotel, and odds were that they hadn't saved my room. I muscle-tested: *Should I go to the larger, posher hotel my friend had booked, which I knew would be open?* I got a firm No. I didn't believe it, so I asked again. No. *Should I go to my hotel?* Yes. *Really?* Yes. *You're sure?* Yes. The muscle-testing fingers were solid as a rock, leaving little room for doubt, which I was inclined to since I was feeling cranky over the earlier wrong answer. Sure enough, I shouted, "Namaste" only twice before a sleepy-eyed guard came to unlock the gate and show me to my sweet terra-cotta-colored room with its fresh-smelling linens. My friend's hotel was overpriced and dirty, he told me the next day.

So why was the testing so wrong earlier and so right later? It seems to me that, bottom line, there was no real need to know in the airport if the planes were going to fly out. Events were already unfolding, without any help from me, that would get us out of the mountains, and it was more curiosity on my part than anything. I hadn't even been feeling anxious, so there was no need to allay that. But I did have to know about the hotel room, because I was on the verge of making a wrong move. It made one point clear: divining works most powerfully when the question is honest and urgent.

My friend got a different lesson out of it. He had pendled at one point, asking, *Will the plane be delayed by two hours?* He got a Yes—and realized later that his unspoken assumption was that it would be flying after those two hours. Speaking literally, the plane was delayed by two hours, and by another twenty-two as well. His lesson: to be very precise in his wording and careful of unconscious assumptions, a reminder useful to him as a counselor.

SIDESTEPPING PITFALLS

Like a hammer, divining is a tool that can be used wisely or not. Even if you've mastered the practical execution of the divining tools, there are some larger pitfalls that one can easily fall into over time. Most of the pitfalls have to do with the way that we think of divining and what we use it for: for example, we may get a big ego about it, use it to get our way with others, get rigid about the answers, and expect it to save us from all turmoil. You can do much to avoid these pitfalls if you:

Don't Think You're the Amazing One That's Doing It

Divining can do much to diminish the destructive power of the ego, but sometimes it cleverly sneaks in again through the backdoor when we become attached to the process of divining itself or to a particular answer. Or, we can get ego-identified with it—feeling that we have a direct line to the Divine, and all these other poor puzzled souls around us don't, which can actually inflate our sense of self-importance. This is a form of spiritual pride that inevitably brings on corrective action, usually through humiliation!

Don't Rely on It Exclusively

Remember that divining is simply a means of guidance. It is not for everyone or for all situations. Other means of coming to a conclusion are just as valid or more valid in the right time and place. Sometimes in life there is great value in simply sitting down and reasoning something through, carefully and meticulously. Think of divining as one decision-making skill among many, and you'll be more likely to use it when it's wise to do so.

Don't Use It to Try to Control Events and People

Information is power, goes the saying, and a subtle but powerful danger of divining is feeling that accessing information allows us to control the outcome of events in our lives. The truth is that, like a compass, divining will take us where we need to be, but it won't tell us what will happen when we get there. Many more imponderables determine that; we can only guess at those with such words as destiny, karma, synchronicity, God. Divining works for our highest good—which generally does not include making us into top-notch control freaks. In fact, the opposite is more true. Divining loosens our grip on having things always turn out our way, and in that lies real freedom and peace.

Don't Divine Without People's Permission

Trying to get information about your family or friends or neighbors without their permission is unethical and will land you in divining hot water. If you sense that your asking about their thoughts, feelings, intentions, and whereabouts would be upsetting to them, you're probably right. How would you feel in a similar circumstance? Better to ask them directly.

Don't Use It for Medical Diagnosis

Unless you are a trained and certified health practitioner, divining to find a medical diagnosis is not only illegal but dicey. Even for yourself—because who can be neutral about their body?—you're better off talking to a doctor, nurse, osteopath, chiropractor, naturopathic doctor, or other health provider about your symptoms. And absolutely don't do it for someone else, because the risk of a wrong answer can have profound consequences, by either worrying them excessively or making them too complacent.

Don't Get Rigid or Superstitious about the Answers

The process is sacred; the answers are not. They are guidance for you in that exact moment. They give you exactly what you need—in that exact moment. But your needs may change in the next month, week, day, even hour, and so may some of the external factors affecting your question. Move with the Yes or No, but if you see it as a step in a dance rather than words carved in stone, you'll be more in tune with the dynamic, ever-changing nature of the way the Universe works.

Don't Use It to Isolate Yourself

If you're shy, it's all too easy to start divining to learn other people's response toward you: *Does she like me? Did I upset him when I said that?* Alas, this goes under the category of invasion of privacy, and there's a strong chance that our emotions might warp the answers. Instead, ask the person straight out: "How do you feel about me?" "Did I upset you?" Your relationship will most likely flower because you are connecting with them directly and honestly—and who doesn't appreciate that?

Don't Let It Become Overly Serious

The accuracy of divining seems to increase when we're lighthearted—perhaps because the Divine has a great sense of humor. "When we act with those childlike qualities of pure lightheartedness, openness, and playfulness, minus any sarcasm or cynicism, we're matching energies with the Divine and can 'dial in' frequencies of information that are deeper and more true," says psychologist Harvey Schwartz.

Don't Try to Push the River

It is human nature to want things our way, right this very minute, and we may very well try to use divining to whip the future into shape: opening some options, closing others, gunning up the decisions of life like accelerating a speedboat through choppy waters. Because divining is efficient and can ease our way, it may even work to some degree. But ultimately, we have to go through what we're meant to go through, and things don't run on our timetable but on the Divine's, which generally has a much wiser strategy underway. This I learned the hard way when I was unable to rent out my Catskills farmhouse when I left for seventeen months in India. It was a big expense, and months of ads encouraged by anxiety-ridden muscle-testing had proved useless. In India, I negotiated long-distance with an interested couple for two months, but our talks kept stalling out. (I kept getting a Yes for them, even though they only tested at 60–80% positivity.) Finally, I did the chits to see if I should close the house down, pursue seasonal rentals, or let a friend house-sit, and I got *Await another alternative,* followed by *Do no more divination on the house.* Two weeks later, a wonderful couple rented it: they had seen and loved the house three months earlier on Craigslist, but it had taken them that much time to work through logistical matters. Events couldn't move any faster than they did, and the first couple was in effect holding the house for the second. Perhaps if I had asked the right question with muscle-testing, that would have been clear, but I got something more important—another lesson in trust, patience, and divining dynamics.

Don't Expect It to Usher You Past the Abyss

With divining, we may feel we have the world on a string—but as long as we inhabit a body, it can safely be said that, sooner or later, a situation will arise that will bring us to our knees. It may be family, finances, career, romance, health, and it will defy every self-help tool and divining technique we have. That is its great gift to us, because it will drive us, in our desperation, deeper into our core. As the Christian mystic Thomas Merton writes so wisely, "Prayer and love are learned in the hour when prayer has become impossible and your heart has turned to stone."

DEALING WITH DOUBTS

Like everything else in life, divining works most powerfully when you do it with full self-confidence: you're not fighting with yourself as you go along, with one foot on the accelerator and the other on the brake.

With time and practice, you learn to trust the inner voice that tells you you're going down the right road, but along the way, your mind can get very noisy and these larger philosophical questions may rise forcefully:

Am I Blunting My Intuitive Powers?

Don't worry. Intuition—that still, small voice inside—is a necessary part of the divining process. It tells us when and how to ask our questions and what the answers really mean. Some people report becoming more intuitive the more they divine, perhaps because they are more consistently in the alpha state in which intuitive information flows easily. Others, however, report that they don't turn to their intuition as much. Happily, if that happens to too great an extent, that still, small voice will start complaining and—intuitively!—we back away from divining. Also, keep in mind that what many people call intuition is simply their fears, desires, impulses, and conditioning in masquerade—sometimes it's a Mardi Gras in there! The managing mind is crafty in exercising its control, and if we never get an intuitive hit that startles or dismays us, we're probably tuning into the conditioned mind instead. The major clue: intuition has no ego attached to it. It's a simple, quiet knowing free of grasping, self-righteousness, or attitude.

Am I Becoming an Automaton?

Just try it! When we start divining too automatically or mechanically or obsessively, it will go wacky on us and give us odd or inconclusive answers. And we can't overrely on it because of that razor's edge we're walking between trusting 100% but still verifying. Remember, even the top diviners get about 8–10% wrong, and the need to carefully watch feedback from the Universe will keep our mind actively engaged.

Am I Avoiding Personal Responsibility for Decisions?

It depends on how we define ourselves. If we see ourselves as totally autonomous, freewheeling agents in the Universe, then we might logically feel this way. If we see ourselves as essential parts of the greater whole, the question becomes moot, because there is a sense of something larger acting through us, with us, and in us. The word "personal" itself loses its resonance. Ultimately, we are taking responsibility on a much bigger stage—Universal Studios!

EXERCISE
DISSECTING THE DYNAMICS OF DOUBT

Doubt itself has a dynamic that, practically speaking, can affect divining. To understand better how it operates for you personally, try this exercise from author Tom Graves, adapted from his very helpful *The Dowser's Workbook*.

Ask a friend to hide a small object, like a key, in a room. Then go looking for it with pendling or muscle-testing—first, with the assumption that you can't possibly find it; and again, with the assumption that of course you can find it, you're perfect, you're the world's best pendler or muscle-tester. Note down the difference (if any) between the results. Now do it again, without any specific assumptions, but see if you can notice what assumptions arise as you search. Don't worry about them; just notice them, and noticing them, you can allow for their bias in interpreting your results. Watching yourself like this, can you get a sense of being a dispassionate observer, watching you and your assumptions rattling around each other as you work?

What If Your Loved Ones Hate Your Divining?

You're apt to find that the people closest to you will not be happy with your divining. This has been my experience, at least; those closest to me have often been highly critical of this path of mine. A boyfriend called muscle-testing "finger in the hole" and chits "chips," even though, more often then not, the divining deepened and perpetuated the bond between us. But it was also a bone of contention. I think that what bothered him, and my other friends, is the feeling that, in a pinch, I would listen to my divining rather than them. It might be true, at least on occasion, but I see testing not as an outside boss but as an inside truth made manifest. My experience is that it always works out best for all concerned: that is my precondition in divining.

When my friend Barbara Lubow gets accused by family members of using muscle-testing during a disagreement, "I usually apologize because it's true, but inside I think, this answer is going to save a lot of time and effort, and why not? But then again, it's my way of knowing, not theirs," she says.

And that's the crux of it: our way may not be their way. Divining is only one path among many, and it's not for everyone, not at all. So what to do?

- Don't flaunt it. It is a private matter, between yourself and the Divine. It can be more powerful if you don't subject its findings to the critical eyes of others, especially in the beginning as you're finding your footing with it. On the other hand, don't lie about it either; honesty is critical with those we love.

- Don't use it to pry. It's a bad idea to use divining to ask anything about people that they wouldn't want you to know—and you probably know what those questions are. It is an invasion of privacy and an abuse of a sacred tool, and it will have a karmic rebound that will not make you happy.

- Ask their permission to divine when it involves a joint decision that affects both you and your loved one, such as a major move or purchase. If they're opposed to it, use other methods of coming to a decision, as a matter of respect. If they give their permission but specify that it's not necessarily going to be what is ultimately done, accommodate to that.

- Try playing it out. If your loved ones remain strongly opposed to divining, one strategy is to divine on your own, and when the discussion arises about what to do, suggest your solution, without hammering it in or even letting on that it is, well, divinely inspired. Then see whether that solution flies. If it does, you get the secret satisfaction of watching events unfold in uncanny ways. If not, you get another lesson in surrender of the ego—always helpful!

- Try alternating their way with yours if you have differing ideas on a logistical decision, and then compare results. In India, a friend and I had arranged to take a three-hour taxi ride from an ashram to Bangalore, leaving at 8 a.m., but when I muscle-tested, I got that we should leave at 11 a.m. She was not happy with my method, but agreed. (She accused me of "passive bossiness," and I concurred, telling her I was working my way up to "active bossiness.") Then another friend e-mailed me from New York to get the name of our taxi driver to take her from the Bangalore airport to the ashram early that morning. The two schedules exactly dovetailed. He picked her up, drove three hours, dropped her at the ashram, and had an hour break before driving us back. It was for his convenience and monetary gain, apparently, that the muscle-testing counseled our delay.

- Try making a game of it. On something that doesn't really matter—like what highway exit to pull off of to find a good meal—suggest that you both muscle-test to see what happens. When you both come up with a Yes, take that exit and muscle-test for the restaurant. If it's "so far, so good," you can suggest muscle-testing for the entrée—but that might be pushing it!

- Don't get doctrinaire about divining. Remember that at least 8–10% of the time it's wrong, so we can't get too smug. Furthermore, if we do get smug, that percent of inaccuracy will rapidly rise to, oh, 100%. If you find you're superattached to a particular outcome, give yourself a shake and open yourself up to other options. In truth, everything in life is the play of the Divine, and maybe Divine direction is coming out of the mouth of the one you love. At least, be open to the possibility!

What If Your Loved Ones Love Your Divining?

Sometimes the opposite dynamic happens, and your family and friends will be so impressed with your guidance system that they ask you to divine a question for them, too. Or you may kindly offer to help out someone in distress by divining for them.

Resist both temptations! You need solid training and lots of practice to do it accurately for anyone else, and until you're absolutely sure of your skills and are mentally and emotionally clear as a bell, you don't want to get tangled in someone else's decision-making karma. Otherwise, you may find yourself in the dubious position of my friend Annie, who did a tarot reading for a friend who was in love with a man in a failing marriage. On the basis of the cards, Annie advised her to break off the affair. Her friend ignored the advice. She ended up marrying him, they lived together happily, and when he died, he left her many millions. "My disapproval of her dating a married man colored the reading," says Annie ruefully.

Alas, it's all too human of us to see with total clarity how everyone else should live their life, and it's all too easy to cloak our judgments (even from ourselves) as higher truth coming via divining. The best approach is to show others how to muscle-test, pendle, or chit-toss for themselves. Then, as the saying goes, you're teaching them to fish instead of handing them a fish.

If you do divine for someone you're close to, be sure to ask permission first *(May I? Can I? Should I?)* and then consider going the route of blind-testing (see page 132). It will help draw a line so you can separate your emotions and opinions from what the Universe recommends as truly the best course of action for your friend or family member. It may not be the outcome you want; sometimes people learn best the hard way, and efforts we make to ease their trials can thwart their progress.

On the other hand, if a number of people start spontaneously asking you to help them in this way, it might well be a push from the Universe to increase your level of skillfulness; perhaps your role is to be a counselor or helper in this way. Check out the American Society of Dowsers website (dowsers.org) to find books, training programs, and mentors near you so you can do the best job possible.

Children in one's care are another matter, and when it comes to the delicate art of raising them, the use of divining also requires discrimination and balance, especially as they reach the age of twelve or thirteen and start making their own life decisions. "You have to ask first, *Is it okay for me to know this? Is it of value for me to know it? Do I have to let it go without asking any questions?*" says Darlene Van de Grift, the mother of two sons and a daughter, now grown.

Divining about your teenager's questionable friends is fraught with peril for *you:* the fact that you're emotionally involved will distort your results to give you only what you fear—or, if you don't want to face a truth, it may falsely reassure you. A better approach is to work with a divining friend with no attachments to your child to explore all sides of an issue, which you can then hash through some more in conversations with your child.

"Nothing is black or white—there is always more to explore," says Darlene. For example, if your eight-year-old wants to play soccer, testing or pendling may show that it's positive for him or her on the physical, mental, and emotional levels, but on the spiritual level they're doing it to please your spouse and would be more at home in an art program. Discussing it together, you can work out satisfying solutions—perhaps choosing one over the other, doing both, alternating the two, or finding a third option.

EXERCISE
IMPROVING CLARITY

The clearer we are mentally and emotionally, the easier and more lighthearted our days become—and the more powerfully our divining works. What often stands in the way of that clarity are behaviors that we don't like in ourselves, such as envy or aggression—our shadow side—that we innocently and unconsciously project onto others, seeing them as jealous or spiteful toward us. We may then treat them accordingly, which in turn can evoke those very behaviors in them, which then provokes a reaction in us . . . and on and on. It's a basic mechanism of human nature and terribly tricky, and untangling it in ourselves makes great joy and freedom available to us.

The best approach I have found for this is Byron Katie's "The Work." She was an overweight, rage-filled agoraphobic until the day she had a spiritual awakening in a halfway house. With that sudden immersion into Ultimate Reality, she also understood a simple technique to correct self-destructive mental patterns. It involves four questions and a turnaround, which we can apply to any belief or thought that makes us miserable. For example, for the thought, "My mother doesn't love me":

1. Is it true?

2. Can you be absolutely certain that it's true?

3. How do you react when you have this thought?

4. Who would you be without this thought?

Turn the thought around to see if it is as true or truer. ("My mother does love me. I don't love my mother. I don't love myself. My mother doesn't love herself.") Find two or three examples to back up each turnaround.

You can learn more about The Work at thework.com, including videos on topics like parents, money, and career. Two excellent books by Katie are *Loving What Is: Four Questions That Can Change Your Life* and *I Need Your Love—Is That True?: How to Stop Seeking Love, Approval, and Appreciation and Start Finding Them Instead.*

APPENDIX 2

FURTHER RESOURCES

ORGANIZATIONS FOR
MORE TRAINING

All the information in this book is about divining for yourself. If you want to divine for others as a way to help them, it's imperative that you first train with professionals in the field. They will help you not only perfect your techniques, but also identify any personal blocks that could come between you and accurate information.

The American Society of Dowsers is a great resource: its members are generous with their time and expertise. It has annual and regional conferences with a wide range of workshops, local classes, and meetings, as well as a journal. Although dowsing with tools is its main emphasis, it also holds classes on kinesiology and "deviceless dowsing." You can learn more at dowsers.org or by contacting them at American Society of Dowsers, PO Box 24, Danville, VT 05828. Telephone: (802) 684-3417. E-mail: asd@dowsers.org.

The Canadian Society of Dowsers also offers a wide range of helpful services and programs. Contact them at 487 Lynden Road, RR 8, Stn. Main, Brantford, ON N3T 5M1, Canada. Telephone: (519) 647-2257. Email: info@canadiandowsers.org.

Active dowsing organizations exist in many countries, including Kenya, Israel, Mexico, Argentina, and Vietnam. Check the Internet for more details.

Up-to-date information on kinesiology training programs worldwide can be found at the Kinesiology Network website (kinesiology.net). In the U.S., the Energy Kinesiology Association (energyk.org) offers training in a number of kinesiology modalities. Touch for Health Education (touch4health.com) supplies books, workshops, and training CDs on the Touch for Health method of self-healing.

WEBSITES

At whattodobook.com, you'll find more information, including a Q & A, helpful links, and how to find an online divining buddy.

At soundstrue.com, you'll find a rich array of audio resources and books for the inner exploration that divining encourages.

HELPFUL BOOKS

Many good resources are available on divining, personal growth, and spiritual expansion. The following list is only a partial one. You can also, of course, go to a bookstore and divine to find what you need next!

Dowsing and Pendling

There are more than one hundred books on dowsing and pendling in the bookstore of the American Society of Dowsers: dowsers.org/store/index.html; (802) 684-3417.

Many of them can also be found on amazon.com and barnesandnoble.com. Following are some I've particularly enjoyed:

T. Edward Ross and Richard D. Wright, *The Divining Mind: A Guide to Dowsing and Self-Awareness* (Rochester, VT: Destiny, 1990).

Patricia C. and Richard D. Wright, *The Divining Heart: Dowsing and Spiritual Unfoldment* (Rochester, VT: Destiny, 1994).

Together these two stellar, authoritative books take you systematically through the dowsing learning curve, from locating water sources to spiritually healing yourself and the planet.

Tom Graves, *The Diviner's Handbook: A Guide to the Timeless Art of Dowsing* (Colchester: Tetradian, 2008).

———. *The Dowser's Workbook: Understanding and Using the Power of Dowsing* (Colchester: Tetradian, 2008).

Tom Graves and Liz Poraj-Wilczynska, *The Disciplines of Dowsing* (Colchester: Tetradian, 2008).

The first two help you build dowsing skills step-by-step with the aid of practical exercises. The third book skillfully guides you past common pitfalls. Useful and engaging, highly recommended.

Arthur Bailey, *Anyone Can Dowse for Better Health* (Slough: W. Foulsham, 1999). Bailey, past president of the British Society of Dowsers, details how to pendle for food allergies, food, supplements, remedies, and geopathic factors that can create "sick buildings."

Charts

Walt Woods, "Letter to Robin" (downloadable for free at lettertorobin.org or available from the ASD bookstore) is a classic that includes precise directions for programming a pendulum, good pendling instructions, and several charts, including a complicated and valuable "multipurpose form."

Anne Williams, *The Pendulum Book of Charts* (Tower Press, 1984). These and her other charts cover topics ranging from hospital problems to house purchases to hiring employees. Available primarily from the ASD bookstore.

Dale W. Olson, *Pendulum Charts* (Eugene, OR: Crystalline, 2003). Spiral-bound laminated charts on such topics as nutrition, relationship compatibility, and flower essences, as well as percentages, the alphabet, and, of course, a chart to help you select the right chart.

Sig Lonegren, *The Pendulum Kit* (London: Connections, 2000). An all-in-one starter package that includes a pendulum, instruction book, and maps and charts on such subjects as health, weather, foods, and underground water.

Juanita Ott, *Dowse This . . .* (Mirrorwaters, 2008). A series of thick spiral-bound books with charts focusing on subjects such as emotional balance and holistic health.

Muscle-Testing

Touch for Health: The Complete Edition; A Practical Guide to Natural Health with Acupressure Touch and Massage (Camarillo, CA: DeVorss, 2005). A comprehensive illustrated guide to the self-health principles and techniques of the valuable Touch for Health approach.

Machaelle Small Wright offers through her nature research center, Perelandra, a comprehensive set of books, tools, and flower essences. Muscle-testing runs as a theme through them all. More information can be found at perelandra-ltd.com. The following books can also be found in bookstores:

Machaelle Small Wright, *Behaving as if the God in All Life Mattered* (Warrenton, VA: Perelandra, 1997). An autobiographical account of surviving adversity to find spiritual direction.

———. *Perelandra Garden Workbook: A Complete Guide to Gardening with Nature Intelligences* (Warrenton, VA: Perelandra, 1993). A hands-on manual for gardeners who want to communicate consciously with nature intelligence.

———. *Flower Essences: Reordering Our Understanding and Approach to Illness and Health* (Warrenton, VA: Perelandra, 1988). A guide to the use of flower essences for health, with detailed instructions for muscle-testing.

Symbolic Approaches

Joan Bunning, *Learning the Tarot: A Tarot Book for Beginners* (Newburyport, MA: Red Wheel/Weiser, 1998). A popular nineteen-lesson guide that uses a simple spread, the Celtic Cross, to show readers how to uncover what cards mean individually and in relation to each other.

Juliet Sharman-Burke, *The Complete Book of Tarot: A Step-by-Step Guide to Reading the Cards* (New York: St. Martin's/ Griffin, 1996). An accessible, clearly written book that emphasizes the psychological aspects of the Tarot for self-development.

Ralph H. Blum, *The Book of Runes: A Handbook for the Use of an Ancient Oracle* (New York: St. Martin's, 1998). This popular book, which comes with a bag of runes, is a straightforward and modern take on the use of the runes.

Ed Thorsson, *Futhark: A Handbook of Rune Magic* (Rochester, VT: Weiser, 1983). A practical guide from a traditional perspective that explores the history, meaning, and procedures of the runes.

The I Ching or Book of Changes, trans. and ed. by Richard Wilhelm (Princeton: Princeton University Press, 1967). The classic translation of this venerable divination system, it was written by a German scholar of Chinese philosophy. With its poetic structure and thorough explanations, it has withstood the test of time. The illuminating foreword, another classic, was written by Carl Jung.

General Divination

Scott Cunningham, *Divination for Beginners: Reading the Past, Present, & Future* (Woodbury, MN: Llewellyn, 2003). Detailed descriptions of a wide range of divinatory techniques, from natural forces like smoke and birds, to physical objects like mirrors and knives, to symbolic systems like the tarot and *I Ching*.

Sarvananda Bluestone, *Signs of the Times* (New York: Perigee, 1997). A playful book that details seventy-five methods of divination, explains how each has been used historically and culturally, and supplies a simple exercise to explore it.

Barbara Tedlock, *The Woman in the Shaman's Body: Reclaiming the Feminine in Religion and Medicine* (New York: Bantam, 2005). An insightful, lively exploration of shamanism that corrects a scholarly bias by illustrating how women have always been central practitioners of the tradition.

Intuition and Synchronicity

Frances Vaughan, *Awakening Intuition* (New York: Doubleday, 1979). One of the earlier books on intuition and still a classic, it distinguishes between personal and transpersonal intuition and gives practical advice on how to develop it.

Echo Bodine, *A Still, Small Voice: A Psychic's Guide to Awakening Intuition* (Novato, CA: New World, 2001). A down-to-earth book with simple instructions on how to "listen to the gut, not the head."

Charlene Belitz and Meg Lundstrom, *The Power of Flow: Practical Ways to Transform Your Life with Meaning-ful Coincidence*, (New York: Harmony/Three Rivers, 1997). How to recognize synchronicity and live life in such a way that spontaneous coincidences carry you into the ongoing experience of effortless flow. Based on interviews with fifty "flowmasters," it includes twelve practical tools to increase synchronicity and further flow. The website, flowpower.com, includes book excerpts, stories, and a self-quiz.

Ray Grasse, *The Waking Dream: Unlocking the Symbolic Language of Our Lives* (Wheaton, IL: Quest, 1996). This insightful book helps in decoding synchronicities by understanding their underlying symbolic meanings.

Science and the Brain
Malcolm Gladwell, *Blink: The Power of Thinking Without Thinking* (Newport Beach, CA: Back Bay, 2007). An intriguing exploration into the ability of the unconscious mind to make spot-on snap judgments based on "thin slices" of data. He illustrates how overanalysis can stifle that process, as can strong emotions and unexamined assumptions.

Lynne McTaggart, *The Field: The Quest for the Secret Force of the Universe* (New York: Harper Perennial, 2002). A clearly written, lively chronicle of cutting-edge scientific research that points to a unifying energy structure in our universe known as the zero-point field. A good book for nonscientists seeking to understand the implications of quantum theories that are reshaping our world view. Also, in *The Intention Experiment: Using Your Thoughts to Change Your Life and the World* (New York: Free Press, 2008), McTaggart demonstrates the power of intention on machines, plants, animals, and other humans, and establishes a participatory online study of group intention.

Elizabeth Lloyd Mayer, *Extraordinary Knowing: Science, Skepticism, and the Inexplicable Powers of the Human Mind* (New York: Bantam, 2008). A skeptical psychoanalyst explores a century of body-mind research and concludes that supposedly extraordinary paranormal experiences are in fact ordinary and commonly experienced, even if they can't be adequately explained in scientific terms.

Jill Bolte Taylor, *My Stroke of Insight: A Brain Scientist's Personal Journey* (New York: Viking, 2008). A Harvard-trained neuroscientist, Taylor awoke one morning in the midst of a massive stroke on the left side of her brain that left her feeling waves of euphoric bliss even as she realized she was losing her ability to talk, walk, and use her linear-thinking abilities. The book chronicles her recovery and argues that the right brain be allowed more room to operate.

Barry Schwartz, *The Paradox of Choice: Why More Is Less* (New York: HarperCollins, 2004). A thorough, well-documented look how the abundance of consumer and personal choices actually makes decision-making more difficult and stressful, with strategies for diminishing anxiety.

Personal and Spiritual Growth

Judith Blackstone, *The Enlightenment Process: A Guide to Embodied Spiritual Awakening* (St. Paul, MN: Paragon, 2008). In this and *Living Intimately: A Guide to Realizing Spiritual Unity in Relationships* (Sterling, 2002), Blackstone teaches a subtle yet powerful method of nondual meditation. She demonstrates that the more we move toward the Oneness of self-realization, the more individualized and true to ourselves we become. *The Empathic Ground: Intersubjectivity and Nonduality in the Psychotherapeutic Process* (Albany: State University of New York, 2007) is an academic discussion of nondualism useful for therapists and other professionals.

Rick Jarow, *Alchemy of Abundance: Using the Energy of Desire to Manifest Your Highest Vision, Power, and Purpose* (Boulder, CO: Sounds True, 2005). A masterful book with exercises and visualizations that help you dive into your depths so that you can then manifest effectively in the outer world. *Creating the Work You Love: Courage, Commitment, and Career* (Rochester, VT: Destiny, 1995) helps guide you inward through questions and meditations to identify the work that's right for you.

Lucy Jo Palladino, *Find Your Focus Zone: An Effective New Plan to Defeat Distraction and Overload* (New York: Free Press, 2007). If feeling overwhelmed or bored is part of your daily experience, this highly practical book has many useful techniques to help you move through life's routines with a calm, focused, and clear mind.

Flora Courtois, *An Experience of Enlightenment* (Wheaton, IL: Quest, 1986). A small, perfectly charming book in which the author chronicles her spontaneous awakening while a college student in the 1940s.

Joseph Benner, *The Impersonal Life* (Filiquarian, 2007). Written anonymously in 1940, it is a classic among Christian mystical books. Read with a still mind, it will transport you into your depths.

SPIRITUAL MASTERY

I have found the following teachers very helpful on my path, and highly recommend their books, CDs/DVDs, classes, retreats, and teachings. Many of their websites have downloadable audio and video files.

Adyashanti

A Californian trained in the Zen tradition, his teachings combine Buddhism, Hindu Advaita, and Christian mysticism. He is unparalleled at helping you understand what happens to you before, during, and after "waking up" to your true reality.

Website: adyashanti.org

Books: *The End of Your World: Uncensored Straight Talk on the Nature of Enlightenment* (Boulder, CO: Sounds True, 2009).

Emptiness Dancing (Boulder, CO: Sounds True, 2006).

The Impact of Awakening: Excerpts from the Teachings of Adyashanti (Campbell, CA: Open Gate Sangha, 2002).

Byron Katie

Formerly angry and deeply depressed, she had a profound awakening and now teaches a simple method of questioning any disturbing thought with four questions. It cuts like a knife through projections and the tricky nature of mind, opening you up to clarity, deep expansion, and a really happy life.

Website: thework.com

Books: *A Thousand Names for Joy: Living in Harmony with the Way Things Are* (New York: Three Rivers, 2008).

Loving What Is: Four Questions That Can Change Your Life (New York: Three Rivers, 2003).

I Need Your Love—Is That True?: How to Stop Seeking Love, Approval, and Appreciation and Start Finding Them Instead (New York: Three Rivers, 2006).

Who Would You Be Without Your Story? Dialogues with Byron Katie (Carlsbad, CA: Hay House, 2008).

Eckhart Tolle

A former German academician, his depression was the doorway to his sudden, unsought awakening. He speaks from a space of silence with a language so clear and profound that it can touch everyone from angry teens to corporate CEOs.

Website: eckharttolle.com

Books: *The Power of Now: A Guide to Spiritual Enlightenment* (Novato, CA: New World, 2004).

A New Earth: Awakening to Your Life's Purpose (New York: Dutton, 2005).

Hilda Charlton

She was a modern dancer, free spirit, and dedicated seeker of God who spent two decades in India studying with enlightened masters before returning to New York City in 1964. For twenty-three years, she taught joy-filled meditation classes with lessons from the lives of both Christian and Hindu saints.

Website: hildacharlton.com

Books: *Saints Alive* (Woodstock, NY: Golden Quest, 1989).

Hell-Bent for Heaven: The Autobiography of Hilda Charlton (Golden Quest, 1990).

Mooji

A Jamaican who was once a London street artist, he is relentless at putting your feet to the fire with the "Who am I?" question—self-enquiry that helps you glimpse the Ineffable.

Website: mooji.org

Book: *Before I Am: Dialogues with Mooji* (Kochi: Stone Hill Foundation, 2008).

Nisargadatta Maharaj

A cigarette seller in Mumbai with a crusty personality, he had enlightening dialogues with seekers that were captured in *I Am That*. A true classic, it may be the last spiritual book you need.

Book: *I Am That: Talks with Sri Nisargadatta Maharaj* (Durham, NC: Acorn, 1990).

Ramana Maharshi

A beloved sage of India who died in 1950, he had a sudden enlightenment at sixteen, and taught the path to self-realization through silence and asking oneself the single most important question, "Who am I?"

Website: sriramanamaharshi.org

Books: *Talks with Sri Ramana Maharshi* (Tiruvanna-malai: Sri Ramanasramam, 1955).

Be as You Are: The Teachings of Sri Ramana, edited by David Godman (New York: Penguin, 1989).

Sri Sathya Sai Baba

With millions of devotees worldwide, he powerfully emanates unconditional love and vast silence; in his eyes you can glimpse infinity. He teaches the primary importance of love and service, saying, "Hands that serve are holier than lips that pray."

Website: sathyasai.org

Books: John S. Hislop, *Conversations with Sathya Sai Baba* (San Diego, CA: Birth Day, 1979).

Samuel H. Sandweiss, *Sai Baba the Holy Man and the Psychiatrist* (San Diego, CA: Birth Day, 1975).

Jonathan Roof, *Pathways to God: A Study Guide to the Teachings of Sathya Sai Baba* (Faber, VA: Leela, 1992).

ACKNOWLEDGMENTS

This book is in your hands now through the help of many friends and collaborators and much, much grace.

First and foremost, I am grateful to all the people who shared the depth of their experience and wisdom on divining. This book stands on their shoulders. Every person I interviewed from the American Society of Dowsers was more than generous with time and help. Machaelle Small Wright graciously allowed the use of her precise kinesiology instructions. My friends with whom I learned muscle-testing a decade ago—Barbara Lubow, Garnette Arledge, Kathleen Donovan, Lois Slade, Wendy Dompieri—have taught me much about divining through their openness and spiritual growth. Harvey Schwartz was exactly the expansive, lucid source I needed at the exact time I needed it, and Rick Jarow's subtle, sound, and surprising wisdom was invaluable, yet again.

More than thirty friends and family members in the United States and India gave me invaluable feedback on the manuscript, on everything from conceptual clarity to chapter structure to word choice. They include psychologists, educators, dowsers, writers, "mature seekers," and non-seekers. Neal Allen, a reporter with me during my *Bergen Record* days, gave me an astute and thoughtful editing that resulted in me restructuring the book; he's not only a terrific editor but is wise beyond mere words. Jeffrey Williamson gave me a useful cynic's perspective and kindly held my hand while I successfully "shopped" the manuscript at the New York Book Expo. Lucy Jo Palladino helped me clarify key points in defining (so to speak!) the Divine.

I am especially grateful to Tami Simon and her outstanding staff at Sounds True. Their integrity and warmth made publishing this book a joy. Kelly Notaras saw the value in the book and took it on despite my lack of a name, agent, or constituency; Haven Iverson believed in it and edited it with exquisite care and devotion; Jaime Schwalb attended flawlessly to every fine detail.

Heartfelt thanks to Dhanya Komarek, for the initial artwork and her enlightening presence; to Kai Mayerfeld, for her wise input and the spark of inspiration that led to the title; to Pat Hunt, Ana Maria Nicholson, and John Maynard, for their perspicacity and pep talks; to Darlene Van de Grift, for her sage counsel at timely moments; to Suzie Rodriguez, for her writerly insights and unflagging support; to Charlene Belitz, for teaching me how to write a respectful self-help book—her expansiveness and trust inform much of this book; and to Judith Blackstone, whose focus on truth rather than popularity keeps me on target.

Last but far from least, a deep bow to my beloved teachers: Sri Sathya Sai Baba, Ramana Maharshi, Hilda Charlton, Byron Katie, Adyashanti, Mooji—and every person and thing that has been put in front of me. With all my heart, my deepest gratitude for showing me what is next, and next, and next.

NOTES

CHAPTER 1: DIVINING

1 Barry Schwartz, *The Paradox of Choice: Why More Is Less* (New York: Harper, 2004), 99–217.

2 A. Dijksterhuis and others, "On Making the Right Choice: The Deliberation-without-attention Effect, *Science,* 311(5763) (2006): 1005–7.

CHAPTER 2: LAMAS, SOLDIERS, PHYSICISTS

1 Barbara Tedlock, "Toward a Theory of Divinatory Practice," *Anthropology of Consciousness* 17, no. 2 (2008): 62–77.

2 "Marines on Operation Divine for VC Tunnels," *Observer,* March 13, 1967. Newspaper published weekly for U.S. Forces in Vietnam.

3 David Bohm, *Wholeness and the Implicate Order* (London: Routledge, 1980).

4 Lynne McTaggart, *The Field: The Quest for the Secret Force of the Universe* (New York: Harper, 2002), 143–59.

5 Dijksterhuis and others. "On Making the Right Choice."

6 Chun Siong Soon, et al., "Unconscious Determinants of Free Decisions in the Human Brain," *Nature Neuroscience* 11 (2008): 543–45, http://www.nature.com/neuro/journal/v11/n5/abs/nn.2112.html.

7 Robert Lee Hotz, "Get Out of Your Own Way," *Wall Street Journal,* June 27, 2008.

8 Hans-Dieter Betz, "Unconventional Water Detection: Field Test of the Dowsing Technique in Dry Zones," *Journal of Scientific Exploration* 9 (1995): 1–43, 159–89.

9 Edith M. Jurka, "Brain Patterns Characteristic of Dowsers as Measured on the Mind Mirror," *The American Dowser* 23, no. 1 (1983).

10 Tedlock, "Toward a Theory of Divinatory Practice."

CHAPTER 4: MUSCLE-TESTING

1 B. Caruso and others, "A Force/Displacement Analysis of Muscle Testing," *Perceptual and Motor Skills* 91 (2000): 68–92.

CHAPTER 5: PENDLING

1 Betz, "Unconventional Water Detection."

CHAPTER 6: THE CRUX OF IT

1 Attributed to Stanley Kubrick, director of *2001: A Space Odyssey* and other award-winning films.

2 R. A. Emmons and M. E. McCullough, "Counting blessings versus burdens: An experimental investigation of gratitude and subjective well-being in daily life" *Journal of Personality and Social Psychology* 84, no. 2 (2003): 377–89.

3 Robert Emmons, *Thanks! How the New Science of Gratitude Can Make You Happier* (New York: Houghton Mifflin Harcourt, 2007).

INDEX

ABOUT THE AUTHOR

 Intrigued by Eastern philosophies, journalist Meg Lundstrom traveled to India in 1987, where she was introduced to divining. It guided her into fruitful meditation practices, deepening experiences of the Divine, romance, a country farmhouse, and purchases as small as silverware and as big as cars. In 1993, divining directed her to Tibet, where she and a friend, Charlene Belitz, experienced a series of synchronicities that led them to write *The Power of Flow: Practical Ways to Transform Your Life with Meaningful Coincidence* (Crown, 1997), which has been published in ten languages.

Lundstrom has written on self-development, health, entrepreneurship, and the human search for meaning, for *Redbook, Business Week, Woman's World,* and other publications. Previously, she investigated Mafia corruption and covered mental health care and other issues for the *North Jersey (Bergen) Record,* and organized successful media campaigns for environmental causes and candidates in Colorado.

She divides her time between the Catskills, Big Sur, and South India.

ABOUT SOUNDS TRUE

Sounds True was founded in 1985 with a clear vision: to disseminate spiritual wisdom. Located in Boulder, Colorado, Sounds True publishes teaching programs that are designed to educate, uplift, and inspire. We work with many of the leading spiritual teachers, thinkers, healers, and visionary artists of our time.

To receive a free catalog of tools and teachings for personal and spiritual transformation, please visit soundstrue.com, call toll-free 800-333-9185, or write to us at the address below:

P.O. Box 8010
Boulder CO 80306